SCHOOL OF AMERICAN RESEARCH PRESS

ARROYO HONDO ARCHAEOLOGICAL SERIES

DOUGLAS W. SCHWARTZ
GENERAL EDITOR

ARROYO HONDO ARCHAEOLOGICAL SERIES

1
The Contemporary Ecology of
Arroyo Hondo, New Mexico
N. Edmund Kelley

2
Prehistoric Pueblo Settlement Patterns:
The Arroyo Hondo, New Mexico, Site Survey
D. Bruce Dickson, Jr.

ARROYO HONDO SITE SURVEY

The publication of this volume
was made possible by a grant from the
NATIONAL SCIENCE FOUNDATION.

PREHISTORIC PUEBLO SETTLEMENT PATTERNS:

THE ARROYO HONDO, NEW MEXICO, SITE SURVEY

D. Bruce Dickson, Jr.

SCHOOL OF AMERICAN RESEARCH PRESS

ARROYO HONDO ARCHAEOLOGICAL SERIES, Volume 2

SCHOOL FOR ADVANCED RESEARCH PRESS
Post Office Box 2188
Santa Fe, New Mexico 87504-2188
www.sarpress.sarweb.org

Douglas W. Schwartz, General Editor
Philip Brittenham, Director of Publications
Jane Kepp, Series Editor

Library of Congress Cataloging in Publication Data

Dickson, D. Bruce.
Prehistoric pueblo settlement patterns.

(Arroyo Hondo archaeological series; v.2)
A revision of the author's thesis, University of Arizona, 1973.
Bibliography: p. 127
1. Pueblo Indians—Antiquities. 2. Indians of North America—New Mexico—
Antiquities. 3. Arroyo Hondo site, N.M. 4. New Mexico—Antiquities.
I. Title. II. Series.
E99.P9D53 1979   978.9′53   79-21542
ISBN 0-933452-02-0

FIG. 1. Aerial View of Arroyo Hondo Pueblo after the Final Season of Excavation

Foreword

In the early years of the fourteenth century A.D. a Pueblo village was established near the rim of Arroyo Hondo, eight kilometers south of present-day Santa Fe, New Mexico (Fig. 1). During the 125 years of its occupation the settlement experienced dramatic changes in population size, changes perhaps shared by other settlements in the northern Rio Grande valley during this critical phase in the region's culture history. A few of the fourteenth-century pueblos survived and are still active today in locations near their original sites. Many more, like Arroyo Hondo, were abandoned prehistorically. Why some of these towns survived and others failed, what caused their population growth or decline, and how these changes affected their way of life were focal questions for the archaeological work carried out by the School of American Research at Arroyo Hondo Pueblo.

Test excavations were undertaken on Arroyo Hondo Pueblo in July, 1970, followed by full-scale excavations during the summers from 1971 through 1974, in addition to ecological and archaeological surveys of the surrounding area. The National Science Foundation supported the project with grants GS–28001 and GS–42181. Laboratory processing took place during the winter months, along with research on the literature pertaining to the relationship of demographic and cultural change. The project's preliminary results were published in three field reports (Schwartz 1971, 1972; Schwartz and Lang 1973). After completion of

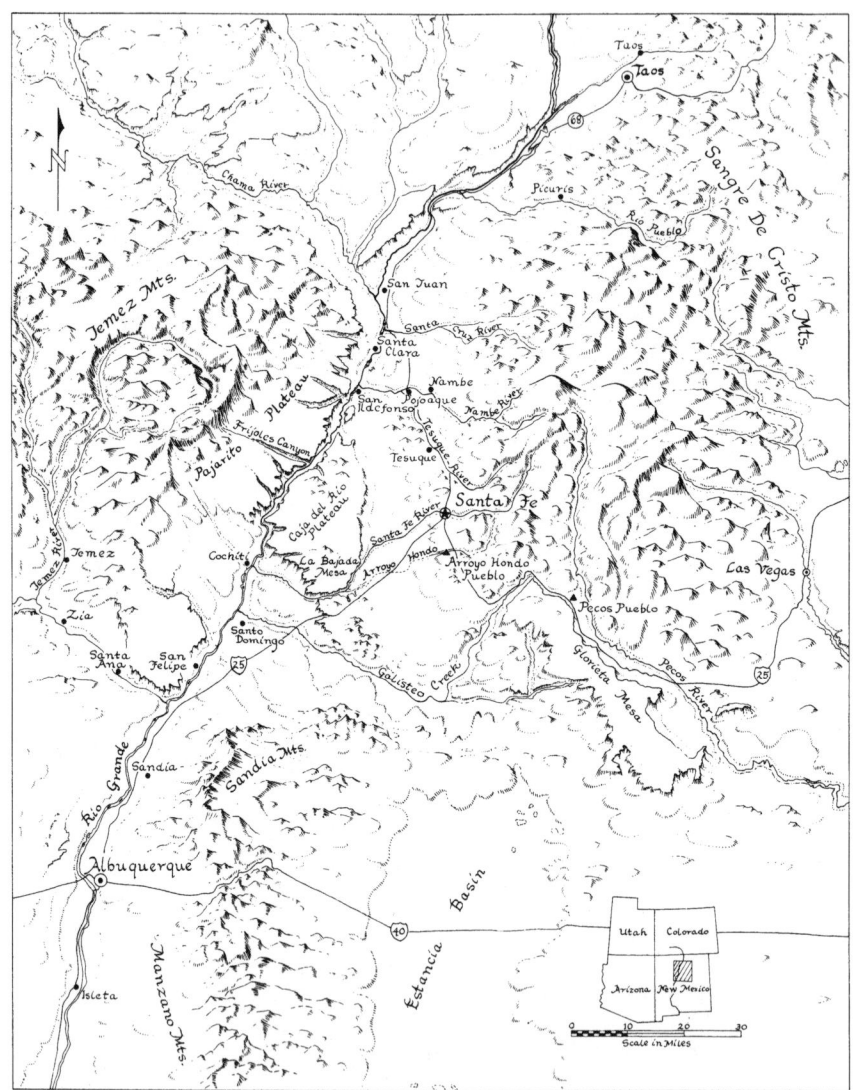

MAP 1.   Location of Arroyo Hondo Pueblo in the Northern Rio Grande Region

the fieldwork, a film, "The Rio Grande's Pueblo Past," was made in collaboration with the National Geographic Society describing the project and presenting a few initial conclusions.

The excavations demonstrated that Arroyo Hondo Pueblo was founded about A.D. 1300 by a few families who built one or two small roomblocks. Following this initial settlement, the town grew rapidly until by A.D. 1330 it covered nearly 6 acres and included 24 roomblocks around 10 plazas. During the middle of the fourteenth century, the pueblo underwent an equally rapid depopulation and was virtually abandoned. Sometime in the 1370s, a new occupation began. The town was partially rebuilt but this time contained only 9 roomblocks around 3 plazas. Arroyo Hondo Pueblo was permanently abandoned about A.D. 1425.

During the course of the project it became clear that the amount of archaeological material recovered and the complexity of the ideas emerging called for publication. A series of ten volumes was planned, nine to present information and ideas on specific topics and one to serve as a final synthesis volume. Although each of the first nine volumes focuses on a particular set of data, it is also intended that each will stand independently in terms of its contribution to northern Rio Grande archaeology as a comprehensive presentation of descriptive data or as an analysis of those data, or as both. Each specialized topic was assigned to one or two individuals who compiled and analyzed the data, in many cases beginning at the fieldwork stage, and who wrote the monograph on that topic.

This book contains the second volume in the series, which has been made possible by an additional National Science Foundation grant (BNS76–82510 A02) for publication development. The topics of the other Arroyo Hondo monographs and their authors are:

Contemporary Ecology, by N. Edmund Kelley
Architecture, by John D. Beal
Ceramics, by Richard W. Lang
Lithic artifacts, by Laurance Linford
Bone, shell, and other artifacts, by Marshall A.
    Beach, Christopher Causey, and Tamsin Venn
Skeletal and mortuary remains, by Ann M. Palkovich
Paleoethnobotany and nutrition, by Wilma Wetterstrom
Paleoecology, including:
    Pollen analysis, by Vorsila Bohrer

Dendroclimatology, by Martin R. Rose, Jeffrey
S. Dean, and William J. Robinson
Faunal remains, by Richard W. Lang and Arthur
H. Harris
Project synthesis, by Douglas W. Schwartz.

The synthesis volume places the site in historical perspective within its larger northern Rio Grande context, integrates the contributions of the preceding volumes in terms of the culture and dynamics of the pueblo, and addresses the broader questions of the relationship between rapid population growth and cultural change.

THE ARROYO HONDO SITE SURVEY

The culture history at Arroyo Hondo Pueblo can be best understood against the broader context of the cultural sequence in the northern Rio Grande valley, which is the subject of this volume. Bruce Dickson's work focused on two main problems: (1) the extent of the pueblo's territory as indicated by the distribution of nearby, contemporaneous communities and (2) the way the settlement and abandonment of Arroyo Hondo Pueblo relate to the general pattern of northern Rio Grande prehistory.

Dickson approached these problems through a field survey and research on previously recorded sites in the Arroyo Hondo area. The project resulted in Dickson's Ph.D. dissertation for the University of Arizona Department of Anthropology (1973); a summary of his dissertation has already been published (Dickson 1975). This volume describes the survey project in full and presents a stimulating model of the relationship between natural-resource distribution and settlement change through time in the northern Rio Grande region. Therefore, just as Kelley's earlier work in this series (1980) laid a solid foundation for understanding the ecology of the Arroyo Hondo region, Dickson in this volume has provided valuable and creative insights that allow the cultural and historical dynamics of the pueblo to be seen as part of a larger system that includes environment, culture, and population.

Douglas W. Schwartz

xii

REFERENCES

DICKSON, D. BRUCE, JR.
1973   "Settlement Pattern Stability and Change in the Pueblo Cultures of the
        Middle Northern Rio Grande Area, New Mexico," (Unpublished Ph.D.
        dissertation, University of Arizona, Tucson).
1975   "Settlement Pattern Stability and Change in the Middle Northern Rio
        Grande Region, New Mexico: A Test of Some Hypotheses," *American
        Antiquity* 40:159-71.
KELLEY, N. EDMUND
1980   *The Contemporary Ecology of Arroyo Hondo, New Mexico,* Arroyo Hondo
        Archaeological Series, vol. 1 (Santa Fe: School of American Research Press).
SCHWARTZ, DOUGLAS W.
1971   *Background Report on the Archaeology of the Site at Arroyo Hondo: First
        Arroyo Hondo Field Report* (Santa Fe: School of American Research).
1972   *Archaeological Investigations at the Arroyo Hondo Site: Second Field
        Report-1971* (Santa Fe: School of American Research).
SCHWARTZ, DOUGLAS W., AND RICHARD W. LANG
1973   *Archaeological Investigations at the Arroyo Hondo Site: Third Field
        Report-1972* (Santa Fe: School of American Research).

CONTENTS

Foreword
    by Douglas W. Schwartz, General Editor   ix
Acknowledgments   xix

1. INTRODUCTION   1
    Survey Objectives and Research Design   2
    The Middle Northern Rio Grande Sequence   4
        Developmental Period (A.D. 600–1200)   10
        Coalition Period (A.D. 1200–1325)   12
        Classic Period (A.D. 1325–1610)   13
        Discussion   14

2. MECHANICS OF THE SURVEY PROJECT   17
    Establishment of the Survey Areas   17
    Site Survey Field Procedures   19
    Artifactual Analysis   20
    The Site Weight Index   22

3. SURVEY RESULTS   29
    Preceramic and Developmental Periods   29
    Coalition Period   32
    Classic Period   34
    Historic Period   35
    Population History of the Study Area   36

4. THE MODEL OF SETTLEMENT PATTERN CHANGE   43
    Definition and Description of Natural Districts   44
        The Rio Grande Floodplain and Terraces   48
        The Santa Fe River Canyon   52
        The Upper Arroyo Hondo Canyon and the Western
            Foothills of the Sangre de Cristo Mountains   54
        Tetilla Canyon   57

    The Middle Arroyo Hondo Drainage   58
    The Canyon at the Edge of La Bajada Mesa   60
    The Remaining Area of the Transect   61
  The Model of Settlement Change   62

5. CONCLUSIONS   67
  An Interpretation of Arroyo Hondo Pueblo Prehistory   67
  An Interpretation of Northern Rio Grande Prehistory   70

Notes   78

Appendices
A. Delineation of the Arroyo Hondo Sustaining Area   79
B. Basic Site Data (Tables 5–7)   87
C. Ceramic Inventory from the Arroyo Hondo
       Archaeological Survey   111
D. Sites Immediately Beyond the Sustaining Area and Transect 117

References   127

MAPS AND FIGURES

Maps

1 Location of Arroyo Hondo Pueblo in the
     Northern Rio Grande Region   x
2 The Study Area: The Hypothetical Sustaining Area
     and the Survey Transect   5
3 The Natural Districts Recognized in the Study Area   46
4 The Proposed Arroyo Hondo Sustaining Area   83

Figures

1 Aerial View of Arroyo Hondo Pueblo after
     Final Season of Excavation   viii
2 Relative Population Magnitudes Through Time in
     the Transect, Sustaining Area, and Study Area   40
3 Natural District 1: The Rio Grande Floodplain
     and Terraces   50

Contents

4   Natural District 2: The Santa Fe River Canyon   52
5   Natural District 3: Upper Arroyo Hondo Canyon
        and the Western Foothills of the Sangre de
        Cristo Mountains   55
6   Natural District 5: The Middle Arroyo Hondo
        Drainage   59
7   Natural District 6: The Canyon at the Edge of
        La Bajada Mesa   60

TABLES

1   Cultural Sequence and Site Weight Totals in
        the Study Area   37
2   Cultural Sequence and Site Weight Totals in the
        Arroyo Hondo Pueblo Sustaining Area   38
3   Cultural Sequence and Site Weight Totals in the
        Survey Transect   39
4   Cultural Sequence and Site Weight Totals in the
        Six Natural Districts in the Study Area   47
5   Sites in the Study Area   87
6   Site Components by Period and Phase in the
        Study Area   98
7   Site Components by Period and Phase in the Six
        Natural Districts in the Study Area   106

Acknowledgments

This monograph is a revised version of my doctoral dissertation, which was submitted in 1973 to the University of Arizona. The study emerged from a site survey done under the sponsorship of the School of American Research in Santa Fe, New Mexico, as part of the School's Arroyo Hondo Pueblo archaeological project, supported by the National Science Foundation. Dr. Douglas W. Schwartz, president of the School and principal investigator of the Arroyo Hondo project, provided me with research latitude, scholarly criticism, professional advice, and warm personal friendship, all of which are greatly appreciated. I wish also to express my gratitude to my committee chairman, Dr. T. Patrick Culbert, for his sustained guidance, both scholarly and practical, and for his good humor and strong encouragement throughout. Special thanks are also due to Dr. Arthur J. Jelinek for his meticulous and insightful criticism at various stages in this work and for his rigorous scholarly example.

In addition, the other members of my committee, Dr. William A. Longacre, Dr. Emil W. Haury, Dr. Keith H. Basso, and the late Dr. Edward P. Dozier, all contributed a great deal of advice and criticism that I found most profitable. Stewart Peckham, David Snow, and the staff at the Laboratory of Anthropology of the Museum of New Mexico extended me exceptional cooperation, advice, and friendship throughout this study and gave me complete access to the site files and information in their charge.

A great debt is owed to two coworkers on the Arroyo Hondo project. Richard W. Lang analyzed the ceramics from my survey as part of his overall study of the material recovered at Arroyo Hondo Pueblo and commented extensively on my dissertation prior to this publication. Edmund Kelley, staff ecologist on the Arroyo Hondo project, provided me with insight and information on the ecology of the middle northern Rio Grande region during the course of our mutual field survey work. Dr. Prentise M. Thomas of the University of the Americas and Dr. Stuart Struever of Northwestern University are also thanked for commenting on parts of the manuscript.

The illustrations in this volume are credited to David G. Noble, who took and printed all the photographs, and Richard W. Lang, who drew all the maps and the graph in Figure 2.

My wife Mary Ann's part at all stages of this undertaking has been enormous. Variously, she has been critic, advocate, and research assistant. At times, with our eldest daughter, she has been a companion in the field. Without her, this work would have been impossible, and it is to her that it is dedicated.

1

Introduction

On entend rétrospectivement quand on a compris.
                                                   —Proust

The archaeological survey reported here was conducted between June and November, 1971, under the auspices of the School of American Research. The work was done in conjunction with, and as a complement to, the Arroyo Hondo archaeological project, a 4-year, interdisciplinary research program at Arroyo Hondo Pueblo, about 4½ miles south of the Plaza of Santa Fe, New Mexico (see Map 1, p. x).

Three core notions are at the base of this study. The first is that the distributions of human settlement through space and time are not random phenomena but are governed by certain physical and cultural constraints that are as yet only partially understood. The second is that principles of animal and plant ecology, specifically those that deal with population succession, bear on the problem of accounting for these variations in human settlement through space and time. The third is that since they involve fairly large numbers, site distributional "counts," like lithic and ceramic counts, are best dealt with through the application of statistical and computer methods; site survey data should therefore be collected in such a manner as to facilitate such application.

The site survey work on which this study is based was undertaken to provide a picture of Arroyo Hondo Pueblo's place in its surround-

1

ing social and physical environment, information that is essential to the project's goal of filling out the culture history of the middle northern Rio Grande region. In addition, the work at and around Arroyo Hondo was viewed as an attempt to apply data and archaeological perspective to the more general problems of demographic and cultural change. That is, the archaeological work at Arroyo Hondo was designed to test and refine certain hypotheses concerning demography and cultural change and to generate additional hypotheses.

Both of these major objectives required a regional perspective that the excavation of a single site could not provide. Therefore, an archaeological site survey was undertaken to delineate "the culture and population history of a sample portion of the Northern Rio Grande area" (Schwartz 1970:3), of which Arroyo Hondo Pueblo is a part. In addition to this delineation, we hoped to obtain information about both the regional demographic pattern in general and the particular sites that related and contributed population to Arroyo Hondo Pueblo after A.D. 1300. It was assumed that to understand fully the cultural changes brought about at the Arroyo Hondo site by the influx of people to that location, it would be necessary to have a fairly detailed knowledge of the regional system of settlement patterning before, during, and after the period of the site's occupation.

SURVEY OBJECTIVES AND RESEARCH DESIGN

The first priority of our 1971 site survey was to examine the pueblo's immediate surroundings in order to locate neighboring sites and to define the "sustaining area," or area from which Arroyo Hondo Pueblo had drawn its primary sustenance (see Appendix A, p. 79). To these ends, an intensive survey was undertaken of an area of approximately 18 square miles centering on Arroyo Hondo Pueblo. This effort, which began in June and lasted until mid-July of 1971, constituted the first phase of the Arroyo Hondo Pueblo site survey project.

The second phase of this project had its intellectual origins in the library research done before fieldwork began. At that time, I was struck by the apparent similarity between the site distributions reported from some parts of the northern Rio Grande by Smiley,

Stubbs, and Bannister (1953:map) and Wendorf (1953:94) and those observed by Adams (1962:112–13) and Hole, Flannery, and Neely (1969:355–56) in the Khuzistan region of Iran. These Khuzistan scholars indicate that through time a gradual downward movement of settlement to lower and lower elevations occurred in Iran. The earliest agricultural settlements tended to cluster in the piedmont regions of the Mesopotamian basin, where the rainfall was relatively high; the greatest number of sites occupied after about 5000 B.C. tended to be on the actual floodplains of the Tigris and Euphrates rivers. Since the low rainfall of the floodplain proper renders dry farming impossible, Adams concluded that this gradual downward movement was due to the increased use of irrigation agriculture over the dry farming methods used earlier in the piedmont.

The available literature for the northern Rio Grande area likewise seemed to suggest that the earlier sites were clustered in the piedmont and away from the semiarid floodplain of the Rio Grande. However, after about A.D. 1325, there appeared to be a general abandonment of the piedmont in favor of the Rio Grande floodplain and some of its major tributaries such as the Galisteo Creek (Smiley, Stubbs, and Bannister 1953:map; Wendorf 1953). It seemed plausible that here, as apparently was the case in Khuzistan, the primary drainage could not be settled successfully until after effective irrigation techniques were developed or imported and that prior to that time settlement was limited to the piedmont area where dry farming, *akchin* farming, or simple floodwater farming (Hack 1942:26–34) could be practiced.

Since it was impossible, on the basis of existing data, to determine whether these general similarities between Iran and the Rio Grande region were more apparent than real, it was decided that the problem would be investigated as part of the 1971 site survey effort in conjunction with the Arroyo Hondo project. The problem was set out as a series of hypotheses of correlation, together with their null hypotheses, and a set of test implications for each. By formally stating the problem as a system of hypotheses, a preliminary, testable model describing settlement pattern change in the middle northern Rio Grande was generated.

The model and its component hypotheses are presented in full elsewhere (Dickson 1975) and will not be repeated here. However, fieldwork was structured around the recovery of data needed to test the hypotheses. Specifically, the test implications demanded that we examine a wide band, or transect, of territory between the piedmont and the Rio Grande in order to isolate any indication of the kinds of settlement changes from higher to lower elevations that were hypothesized to have occurred (Map 2). This transect was examined in terms of a stratified random sample, and the results were examined for evidence of correlation through the use of the phi coefficient statistic.

The results of these statistical tests indicated very strongly that there was *not* a correlation between temporal and spatial place-ment of sites in the middle northern Rio Grande transect area like that observed in Khuzistan. The results were not entirely negative, however, since an alternative placement of sites in time and space that became apparent in the course of our work led to the development of an alternative model and to the generation of a new concept, that of the "natural district," which will be de-fined later. The alternative model proved useful in interpreting middle northern Rio Grande prehistory, particularly in regard to the Arroyo Hondo site, and is amenable to similar testing elsewhere. Presentation of this model and the survey data is the chief purpose of this monograph.

THE MIDDLE NORTHERN RIO GRANDE SEQUENCE

Although this research is not directly concerned with the prob-lems involved in the establishment or refinement of the northern Rio Grande cultural sequence, the work reported here is based on previous research concerned with such problems. Therefore, the development of the cultural sequence in the northern Rio Grande will be discussed briefly in this context.

According to Wendorf, the northern Rio Grande region is "a roughly rectangular area extending from a line through Isleta in the south, and the Colorado line on the north; and from the Canadian River on the east, to the Rio Puerco and Rio Chama on the west" (1954:200). Wetherington (1968:73) subdivides this region into four dis-tinct subregions, or "districts," and lists two other areas as possibly dis-tinct enough to merit separate treatment. The four districts are the Chama River area, the Taos area, the Santa Fe area, and the

4

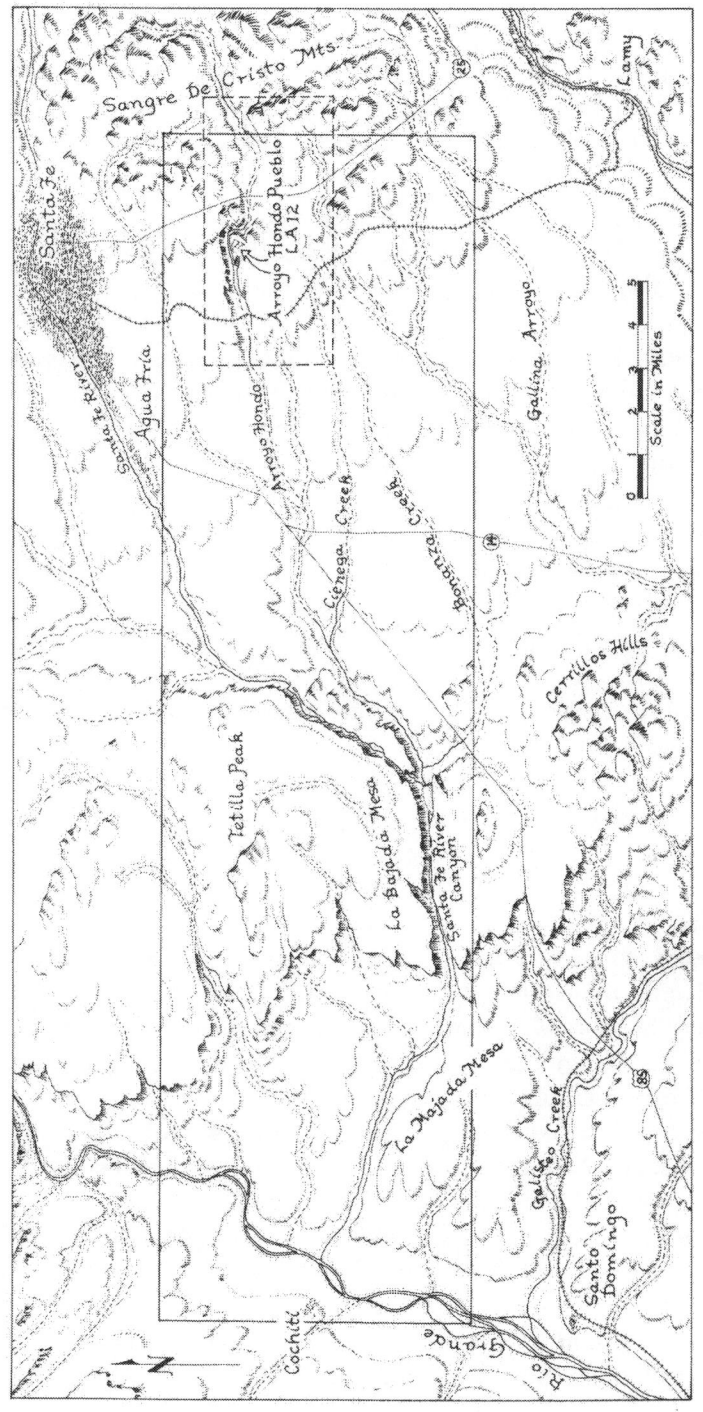

MAP 2. The Study Area: The Hypothetical Sustaining Area and the Survey Transect

5

Albuquerque area. The two provisional districts are the Galisteo basin and the Pajarito and Jemez plateaus. Wetherington specifically describes the Santa Fe district as "bordered by the Rio Grande on the west, the Rio Pueblo on the north, the Pecos River on the east, and on the south by the Galisteo Creek."

We are concerned here with a somewhat smaller area within Wetherington's Santa Fe district. Since we view the events on the Pecos and Galisteo rivers as being distinct from those in the vicinity of Santa Fe, the area we have termed the middle northern Rio Grande is bordered on the east by the Sangre de Cristo Mountains and on the south by a point approximately midway between the Santa Fe and Galisteo rivers, rather than by the Pecos and Galisteo as in Wetherington's scheme.

Although the antiquities of the northern Rio Grande region were known and noted by travelers and military men from the early days of settlement (e.g., Simpson 1850), scientific treatment of ruins did not begin until the late nineteenth and early twentieth centuries, with the work of Adolph Bandelier, Edgar Lee Hewett, and Nels Nelson. Of these, the work of Nelson had perhaps the greatest significance for modern southwestern archaeology. Not only did his extensive "testing" of numerous ruins in and around the Santa Fe area form the basis for much of the subsequent archaeology there but also his pioneering application of stratigraphic analysis laid the groundwork for the general sequence of ceramics and cultural periods in the northern Rio Grande region (Nelson 1914[1]:1–24).

The work of A. V. Kidder at Pecos Pueblo built on Nelson's research. Pecos also came to assume an importance in Rio Grande and southwestern archaeology beyond the significance of the site itself. It was here in 1927 that the first Pecos Conference was held and the basic sequence of Anasazi cultural stages was formulated. The southwestern cultural paradigm that emerged at this conference divided the prehistory of the area into a sevenfold sequence, beginning with the Basketmakers and ending with fully developed Pueblo culture (Kidder 1927).

Archaeological work in the northern Rio Grande following the first Pecos Conference largely involved chronological placement of new sites within the Pecos classification. The work of H. P. Mera is classic in this regard. Mera closely concentrated on problems of ceramic minutiae to the near exclusion of other cultural elements.

6

However, through the systematic use of these ceramic data, he attempted to correlate prehistoric cultural complexes with modern language groups in the Rio Grande (1935:36–39) and was among the first to consider the problem of population change in the area (1940). Mera was also among the first to note systematically the similarities in design and manufacture of northern Rio Grande ceramics to the ceramics of Chaco Canyon (1935:3,5) and, later, to those of Mesa Verde (1935:22). His conclusion that these similarities, at least in the latter case, indicated migration from the Four Corners area assumed the status of a basic premise in much of the later work in the Rio Grande (e.g., Reed 1949; Riley 1952; Stubbs and Stallings 1953; Wendorf 1954). Although the phase system he proposed (Mera 1935), together with some of his correlations between language and culture, has been largely rejected, Mera's meticulously ordered ceramic work placed northern Rio Grande prehistory on a firm footing.

The work of Stubbs and Stallings in the 1930s is more difficult to assess, primarily because only a few of the sites they excavated were ever reported in publications and many of the unpublished manuscripts were lost to science for a variety of reasons. However, sufficient data existed to allow T. L. Smiley and B. Bannister of the Laboratory of Tree-Ring Research of the University of Arizona to work with Stubbs and publish material that firmly and systematically dated some key sites in the Rio Grande area (Smiley, Stubbs, and Bannister 1953). Stubbs also published an account of the work at Pindi Pueblo, which remains the type site of the Coalition Period in the northern Rio Grande (Stubbs and Stallings 1953).

More important to this discussion, Stubbs (in Smiley et al. 1953:56–62; Stubbs and Stallings 1953:152–55) proposed a cultural sequence for the Rio Grande that differed somewhat from the Pecos classification applied to the area up to that time. The most substantial variation from that taxonomy was the combination of the Anasazi Pueblo I and Pueblo II into the single Developmental Period. Cultural growth in the Rio Grande was seen to be part of the general "San Juan–Chaco" expansion and cultural development during these years but to be insufficiently differentiated in the northern Rio Grande to warrant the twofold division (Stubbs in Smiley et al. 1953:60). For the remainder of the sequence, the Pecos classification was retained.

In the years since its formulation, the Pecos system has been increasingly regarded as inapplicable, at least in its totality, outside the Four Corners region (Wendorf and Reed 1955:133–34). Soon after assuming the directorship of the Laboratory of Anthropology, Fred Wendorf published the first extensive revision in the Rio Grande cultural sequence since the original Pecos classification. This new synthesis marked the effective end of attempts to force the Rio Grande data into a northern Anasazi sequential scheme.

Wendorf combined the sketchy data on Early Man and Archaic occupation in the northern Rio Grande to form the Preceramic or Early Period, which ran from about 15,000 B.C. until A.D. 600 (1954:202). Then, concluding that Basketmaker II sites were absent from the area, he telescoped the Pecos classificatory periods of Basketmaker III, Pueblo I, Pueblo II, and part of Pueblo III into the Developmental Period, which lasted from A.D. 600 to A.D. 1200, while the architectural sequence passed from pithouses to contiguous-walled surface structures (1954:204).

Wendorf termed the following interval the Coalition Period (A.D. 1200 to A.D. 1325), the onset of which was marked by the shift in ceramic manufacture from mineral to organic paint and the appearance of design motifs similar to those of Mesa Verde. Although a similar change had occurred earlier in the Kayenta district of the Anasazi, Wendorf concluded that the shift from mineral to organic paint did not necessarily represent a migration from that region during the first or Pindi Phase of the Coalition (A.D. 1200 to A.D. 1300) but merely indicated increased diffusion from there (Wendorf and Reed 1955:144). However, Wendorf saw evidence of an actual migration from the Four Corners region in the appearance in the northern Rio Grande of large, multistoried pueblos in the Galisteo Phase of the Coalition Period from A.D. 1300 to A.D. 1325 (Wendorf and Reed 1955:145). Thus, Wendorf accepted the notion espoused earlier by Mera, Reed, Stubbs and Stallings, and others that migrants abandoning the San Juan had moved into the northern Rio Grande, causing the "climax area for the Anasazi" to shift from the vicinity of the San Juan to the northern Rio Grande, where it remained until the Historic Period (Wendorf 1954:208).

Wendorf dispensed with Pueblo IV and further divided the prehistory of the area into a Classic Period (A.D. 1325 to A.D. 1600), which was characterized by certain Western Pueblo traits and by the manufacture of distinctive glaze-painted ceramics (Wendorf 1954:213). These Classic developments were interrupted, of course, by the Historic Period, beginning in the seventeenth century and continuing to the present. A year after the publication of his original article, Wendorf collaborated with Erik K. Reed on a slightly revised sequence that left the essentials of the earlier work intact (Wendorf and Reed 1955).

In the years following this synthesis, work in the northern Rio Grande tended to be of a salvage nature and, perhaps of necessity, empirical and nontheoretical. This work did little to modify the theoretical framework; rather, such programs as the Cochiti Dam Archaeological Salvage Project (which, as a strange anachronism, returned to the Pecos classification) tended to confirm the view that there did indeed exist an unbroken sequence of cultural phases in the northern Rio Grande that fit nicely into Wendorf's stages.

Exceptions to this exist, of course. McNutt's account of his excavations at the Tesuque By-Pass salvage site included a general discussion of the northern Rio Grande sequence that differed from Wendorf's to some extent in terminology and culture process. McNutt termed the Developmental Period the Colonization, from about A.D. 750 to A.D. 1225 (1969:113), and he argued against Wendorf's conclusion that the cultural developments during the Pindi Phase of the Coalition Period were due to diffusion rather than migration from the Mesa Verde area (McNutt 1969:98–109). Another notable exception was Wetherington's (1968) initial report on the excavations of the Fort Burgwin Research Center at Pot Creek Pueblo near Taos. Wetherington (1968:86–99) also included a review of northern Rio Grande prehistory, but one more substantive than McNutt's in that it rounded out Wendorf's general paradigm with an explicit division of the region into four subregions or districts with a proposed phase system for each.

The chronological scheme for the northern Rio Grande region upon which this research is based is chiefly a composite of the work of Wendorf (1954), Wendorf and Reed (1955), and Wetherington (1968), with the author's own addition of a Middle Phase to the Coalition Period. However, it is important to stress in this connection that although cultural morphology through time is discussed in the work, I do not define the phases and periods listed below in cultural terms. Instead, periods and phases are here considered to be "units

9

of time, or more specifically, units of contemporaneity" (Rowe 1962:40). That is, they are defined strictly in temporal terms. If two sites in an area were occupied in the same year, they both date to the same period, regardless of whether or not their cultural inventories were identical. With this in mind, the chronological framework of this book is as follows:

Early or Preceramic Period (before A.D. 600)

Developmental Period (A.D. 600–1200)
    Early Phase (A.D. 600–900)
    Middle or Red Mesa Phase (A.D. 900–1100)
    Late or Tesuque Phase (A.D. 1100–1200)

Coalition Period (A.D. 1200–1325)
    Early or Pindi Phase (A.D. 1200–1250)
    Middle Phase (A.D. 1250–1300)
    Late or Galisteo Phase (A.D. 1300–1325)

Classic Period (A.D. 1325–1610)
    Early Phase (A.D. 1325–1400)
    Middle Phase (A.D. 1400–1542)
    Late Phase (A.D. 1542–1610)

Historic Period (A.D. 1610–present)

To provide an overview of northern Rio Grande prehistory, each of the chronological periods as represented in that region will be discussed briefly here. The Early or Preceramic Period and the Historic Period fall outside the scope of our research and therefore are not included in the following sections.

Developmental Period (A.D. 600–1200)

This period is subdivided by Wetherington (1968:88) into three phases, the Early, Red Mesa, and Tesuque, in what that author calls the Santa Fe district and what we term the middle northern Rio Grande region. These phases have been retained in this work but are referred to as Early, Middle, and Late, respectively. The Early Phase of this period lasted from about A.D. 600 until A.D. 900. Wetherington is reluctant to concede that this phase has any validity in the Santa Fe district on the grounds that only one site (Mera's LA 177) from that time range has been mentioned in print and none has been excavated (Wetherington 1968:88). Since his writing, however, two sites with Early Phase components were excavated during the Cochiti Dam project (Lange 1968). A search of the Laboratory of Anthropology site files revealed eight more, and the 1971 site survey uncovered an additional one, for a total of eleven Early Phase sites.

Five of these sites, including Mera's LA 177, produced Lino Gray or Lino Black-on-gray pottery, two others Whitemound Black-on-white, and the remainder an "early" form of Red Mesa Black-on-white, which would place them near the end of the phase (cf. Breternitz 1966:90). Thus, sufficient evidence exists for us to refer to an Early Phase of the Developmental Period in the middle northern Rio Grande region. On the basis of work done here and in the more numerous Early Phase sites in the vicinity of Albuquerque, we can characterize surface manifestations of this phase as small villages of circular pithouse structures with ceramics of the types associated with Basketmaker III and Pueblo I outside the Rio Grande valley.

The Middle or Red Mesa Phase of the Developmental Period was first defined as a phase of the Pueblo II period by Gladwin (1945). It lasted from A.D. 900 to A.D. 1000 and was marked by the transition from pithouses to contiguous-walled adobe surface pueblos. Published data on this phase from the Santa Fe area include the account of the "pre-Pindi" pithouse structure beneath room 164 at Pindi Pueblo (Stubbs and Stallings 1953:25) and the "pithouse occupation in area B" described by McNutt (1969:56). Both Gladwin (1945) and Wetherington (1968) cite Red Mesa Black-on-white ceramics as the dominant painted ware.

The Late or Tesuque Phase of the Developmental Period lasted from A.D. 1000 until A.D. 1200. Data collected during the 1971 site survey seem to substantiate Wendorf and Reed's assertion that the number and size of sites gradually increased during the Developmental Period after A.D. 900 and reached a peak during the Late Phase (1955:140). According to Wendorf and Reed, sites of this phase "range from small ten-to-twelve-room pueblos to fairly large communities of over a hundred rooms, having from one to more than four kivas" (1955:140).

Published accounts of excavated sites from this phase in the Santa Fe area include: the "Kwahe'e Complex" at the Tesuque By-Pass site, which consists of a slab-based roomblock and a D-shaped kiva

11

(McNutt 1969:57); the jacal structure beneath rooms 173 and 175 at Pindi Pueblo (Stubbs and Stallings 1953:24–25); and LA 6462, the single pithouse of this phase found at the later pueblo site near Cochiti Pueblo (Lange 1968:62). According to Wetherington, the diagnostic ceramic type of this phase is a "local indigenous ware, Kwahe'e Black/White, which appears to derive from its Chaco predecessor with designs in mineral paint strongly reminiscent of Escavada Black/White in the western Anasazi regions" (1968:90).

Coalition Period (A.D. 1200–1325)

Following Wendorf and Reed (1955), Wetherington divides the Coalition Period in the Santa Fe district into two phases, the Pindi and the Galisteo. In this work, these phases are regarded as equivalent to our Early and Late phases, and we have, tentatively at least, recognized a Middle Phase.

The beginning of the Coalition Period in the northern Rio Grande was marked by a technical change in black-on-white pottery, in which carbon paint was substituted for mineral paint. Kwahe'e Black-on-white design elements were largely retained, but the new ware was termed Santa Fe Black-on-white; along with the slab metate, which largely supplanted the trough variety, it became the hallmark of the Early and Middle phases of the Coalition Period in the northern Rio Grande (Wendorf and Reed 1955:144–45).

Most scholars, with the notable exception of McNutt (1969:98–109), tend to regard the changes during the Early and Middle phases as local responses to new ideas diffusing into the area from outside the northern Rio Grande. Wetherington puts it well when he says that "the general pattern seems to indicate a stable situation of local settlements participating in a generalized period of cultural growth but at the same time beginning to show some regional differences" (1968:90).

Finally, there was an apparent decline in the number of sites and perhaps a reduction in the size of some others in the middle northern Rio Grande during the Middle Phase of the Coalition. The onset of the Late or Galisteo Phase from A.D. 1300 to A.D. 1325 was marked by a dramatic change in certain areas of northern Rio Grande culture. As noted by Wendorf and Reed (1955:154) and Wetherington (1968:90–91), masonry construction became more common, especially in the Galisteo area; but it did not fully replace puddled adobe at some of the major pueblos in the vicinity of Santa Fe such as Pindi (Stubbs and Stallings 1953:25), Arroyo Hondo, and others. Wendorf and Reed note a change in religious architecture with the appearance at Pindi and other sites of surface kivas, as opposed to subterranean ones (1955:145). Equally striking is the contemporaneous appearance of Galisteo Black-on-white, a ceramic type that shows extremely close affinities with Mesa Verde Black-on-white. In addition to this dominant type, other new wares like Poge, Pindi, and Wiyo Black-on-white also reflected Mesa Verde cultural influence (Wetherington 1968:90).

Classic Period (A.D. 1325–1610)

This period is also subdivided into Early, Middle, and Late phases. The Early Phase (A.D. 1325–1400) is marked by the appearance of Rio Grande Glaze Ware pottery, the date of which is not precisely known. The A.D. 1325 date used here was first suggested by Wendorf and Reed, who noted that glaze ware was present in the upper levels of Pindi Pueblo, dated to A.D. 1349, and absent in the Lamy site dated 1311+ (1955:149). Wetherington prefers the later date from Pindi and begins the Classic Period at A.D. 1350. Breternitz, in his recent calibrations of tree-ring dates and ceramic types, suggests a date around A.D. 1300 for the appearance of Glaze I in the northern Rio Grande (1966:91), although the appearance of glaze ware in the middle northern Rio Grande may have been somewhat later than in the areas farther south.

Thus, the onset of the Classic Period has become somewhat difficult to define. If Breternitz's date is correct, then the use of Glaze I as a time marker for the beginning of the Early Phase of the Classic Period is questionable. Perhaps from the standpoint of dating, it might be simpler to do away entirely with the Late Phase of the Coalition Period and term the span of years from A.D. 1300 to A.D. 1400 the Early Phase of the Classic Period instead. By doing this we would be able to use the appearance of Galisteo Black-on-white *and* Rio Grande Glaze I as ceramic type-fossils for the Classic Period. However, for the sake of convenience, Wendorf's Late or Galisteo Phase of the Coalition Period has been retained here as dating to between A.D. 1300 and A.D. 1325.

In any case, the Early Phase of the Classic Period was also characterized by the appearance of certain Western Pueblo traits, such as extended inhumation and rectangular kivas. The adoption of these traits in the northern Rio Grande, together with the discovery of glaze decoration on the red-slipped ceramics from the Zuni and Little Colorado areas near the end of the thirteenth century, seems to indicate that ties between these two regions became closer (Wendorf and Reed 1955:149–50).

The subsequent Middle Phase of the Classic Period (A.D. 1400 to A.D. 1542) was marked by the disappearance of Galisteo Black-on-white ceramics and the appearance of Glaze II, both developments that seem to have occurred around the beginning of the phase (Breternitz 1966:76,91). This phase also witnessed the decline of Glaze I after about A.D. 1425 and of Glaze II around A.D. 1500 (Breternitz 1966:91–92). Glaze III, which Breternitz dates between A.D. 1425 and A.D. 1500 or 1550, serves as a ceramic time marker as well, and its disappearance may be used to date the closing of the phase (1966:92). However, the event that officially signifies the end of the phase is the arrival of the Spanish explorer Coronado.

The Late Phase of the Classic Period (A.D. 1542–1610) is bracketed in the middle northern Rio Grande by two events: Coronado's explorations and the founding of Santa Fe in 1610. In terms of ceramics, Glaze V seems to span this phase and last into the first half of the seventeenth century in the Historic Period (Breternitz 1966).

Discussion

While accepting Wendorf and Reed's (1955) chronological framework of cultural periods in the northern Rio Grande, some recent scholars are reluctant to accept all of their explanations of the processes by which the changes in culture that characterized these periods were brought about.

The notion of migration as an adequate explanation has especially been questioned. For example, work by W. James Judge on Early Man (1973) and T. R. Reinhart (1968) and others on Archaic and Basketmaker sites seems to indicate that, in fact, the Rio Grande valley was not as chronically underpopulated as early research suggested. Further, Reinhart's early radiocarbon dates from Rio

Rancho Phase Basketmaker sites near Albuquerque indicate the appearance of the Basketmaker complex of traits in the Rio Grande prior to their appearance in Durango, Colorado. This opens the possibility that the Rio Grande, at least in the first millennium, was not simply a passive receptor of trait complexes from the north but may have, in fact, taken part in their original development and northern transmission (Reinhart 1968).

The possible presence of a substantial nonagricultural, or partially agricultural, population in the northern Rio Grande during the Late Preceramic Period and the Early Phase of the Developmental Period lends strength to the notion that cultural development and population growth there during the subsequent Middle and Late phases of the Developmental Period were due chiefly to *in situ* development. Schoenwetter and Dittert (1968:49,50) cite Carter's (1945) belief that improved strains of maize came into use over much of the Anasazi area after A.D. 700 and hypothesize that such an improvement in the subsistence base was of crucial importance in the gradual increase in certain Anasazi populations after that date. If one could demonstrate that improved, higher yielding maize was also being grown in the northern Rio Grande shortly after A.D. 700, it might be unnecessary to explain the increase in population in that region by invoking the deus ex machina of migration from outside the valley.

As for the presence there during the Developmental Period of certain Chacoan culture traits and styles, Glassow also suggests we cease such invocations and construct instead what he calls explanatory models involving "interaction spheres spanning large segments of the northern Southwest. These interaction spheres may have served as information pools into which Rio Grande societies dipped as various stress situations demanded new style or technology" (1971:226). Such an approach allows us to hypothesize that with the decline and abandonment of Chaco Canyon this interaction between the northern Rio Grande and surrounding Anasazi groups was transferred to the Four Corners region. This development might have led to the corresponding appearance of the Mesa Verde ceramic and architectural styles, of which so much has been made in the past.

In any case, like the recent work of Glassow, Schoenwetter and Dittert, and others mentioned only briefly here, the research reported in this volume is concerned with the processes within and behind the sequential changes in culture form detailed by earlier investigators like Wendorf and Wetherington. Thus, our research accepts the details of the changes described by these earlier authors and seeks to generate hypotheses that will eventually lead to the testable explanations of those changes.

2

Mechanics of the
Survey Project

ESTABLISHMENT OF THE SURVEY AREAS

The 1971 survey was designed to serve two ends: to investigate the hypothetical model of settlement pattern change in the middle northern Rio Grande area in general and to determine the nature of the sustaining area of the Arroyo Hondo site in particular (Appendix A). Accordingly, two separate but complementary strategies were developed.

The locality first examined in the survey and the one covered in the most detail was the presumed sustaining area of Arroyo Hondo (Map 2). This area surrounding the site was covered in its entirety on foot with the objective of collecting the three kinds of data considered most relevant to defining "sustaining area": location of agricultural land, proximity of certain lifezones,[1] and the geopolitical makeup of its surroundings. Sites already known in the area were also included in this determination.

The second survey strategy employed during the 1971 field season was used as a means of testing our model of settlement pattern stability and change. In line with the established test implications, a transect between 4 and 6 miles from north to south and 27 miles from east to west was laid out from the eastern edge of the Rio Grande piedmont in the western foothills of the Sangre de Cristo Mountains to the first terrace west of the river (Map 2). This transect covered some 130 square miles of territory, of which 80 square miles, or approximately 62 percent of the total, were actually sur-

17

veyed. The areas surveyed were selected by means of a stratified, random sample whose mechanics are discussed later. This transect, or survey area, runs from east to west across land mapped on the following official U.S. Geological Survey (USGS) quadrangle maps: Seton Village 7.5'; Turquoise Hill 7.5'; and Tetilla Peak 7.5'.

The area within the transect was subdivided into units of 0.25 square mile, or quarter sections, and these units were then sequentially numbered. In all, 253 units were classified on the basis of the available water as shown on the USGS quad maps. The categories used were: (1) watered by perennial streamflow; (2) watered by intermittent arroyo flow; and (3) watered by rainfall only.

Once the transect subunits had been stratified in this manner, samples of varying proportions were taken from each group through use of a table of random numbers. That is, since the strata were listed in order of their decreasing importance to prehistoric (and modern) agriculture and, therefore, generally in order of their decreasing likelihood of containing sites, it was decided that because of time limitations, it would be unprofitable to examine samples of equal size from each group of quarter sections. We came to regret this decision later, as it interjected an element of bias into the sample that could easily have been avoided simply by stratifying the transect more precisely in terms of lifezones as well as available water and then sampling the strata equally.

However, since experience indicated that the presence of perennial water was of key importance to site location, all of the quarter sections exhibiting this feature were examined. It was somewhat more difficult to generalize about the importance of the second stratum, those areas watered intermittently by arroyo flow, especially since many of the recent environmental and hydrological changes in this region make present conditions an uncertain guide to the past. However, although a larger sample would have been desirable, our decision to examine all of the preceding strata left us with sufficient time to survey only 25 percent of this one. Finally, the third category, areas watered by rainfall only, was surveyed to the extent of only 5 percent of its total for the transect. In all, our sampling scheme resulted in a survey of nearly 62 percent of the area within our transect.

A total of 65 previously unknown archaeological sites was recorded during the 1971 survey project. To supplement these data, two additional sources of site information were used. First, the study included 61 sites recorded for the Santo Domingo Pueblo 7.5′ USGS quadrangle map during the Cochiti Dam Archaeological Salvage Project. This area is located at the far western end of our survey area, and by incorporating it we extended the length of the transect from the foothills of the mountains to the Rio Grande floodplain. For the remainder of the transect, the Museum of New Mexico (Laboratory of Anthropology) files were searched; where sufficient data existed, sites were plotted on USGS quadrangle maps for the region, and the information about the sites was recorded. A total of 28 sites was added to the study's sample in this manner. An additional 15 sites are known from the sustaining area, bringing the overall total to 169.

Unfortunately, the kinds of data recorded in the files were not entirely adequate from the standpoint of our research aims. Although generally a site card included the location and a list of the ceramic types represented at the site, most cards contained little or no data on the size of the site, such as the number of structures it comprised or the area it occupied. Thus, we were left with a fairly adequate picture of the spatial and temporal distribution of sites but with little or no indication of their settlement, community, and demographic patterns. Further, in attempting to locate sites recorded in the files, I found that an undetermined number of them had been incorrectly located to some degree. Such a circumstance is certainly understandable considering the absence of accurate maps for much of New Mexico at the time that many of these sites were recorded and the subsequent transfer of data once adequate maps were issued. However, this error factor must be considered in evaluating the recorded site data. Finally, since the system of ceramic classification for the Rio Grande region is still undergoing change and refinement, it seems likely that some of the ceramic classes listed on site cards in the files do not conform to current usage. If this is the case, a certain distortion may have been injected into our temporal assignments.

SITE SURVEY FIELD PROCEDURES

Field survey in the Santa Fe area is both aided and complicated by the fact that the area has been the scene of historic settlement since the early seventeenth century and is currently undergoing a boom in a population and construction. Travel over some of the land to be examined is, of course, facilitated by the bulldozing of new access roads, but such an advantage is offset by the fact that rapid housing development and other construction have sprawled over portions of the survey area far ahead of salvage efforts.This, coupled with the widespread belief that any stranger closely examining undeveloped or untended property is either a realtor or a potential thief, complicates site survey.

I examined the various quarter sections in the sample by crossing and recrossing them in as systematic a fashion as their terrain would permit, using a Brunton pocket transit compass to maintain a uniform course. I conducted survey work on foot, almost always working alone. Following a preliminary examination, I numbered the various surface features at each site, separately bagged the artifacts associated with them, and then made a concerted effort to collect all the other surface artifacts on the site. The limited size of all but 3 of the more than 100 sites discovered or revisited during the survey facilitated this procedure. Each site was then photographed, and using tape and pocket transit, a sketch map was made of the surface manifestations.

On the basis of this surface examination and sketch mapping, the number of structures and rooms for each site was determined or inferred, using surface features such as wall stubs, depressions, and mounds in the calculations. Although many of the sites in the survey area probably contained structures that left no traces on the modern ground surface, there does not seem to be any remedy for the underestimations that this fact injects into our figures. Until someone demonstrates that a mathematically specifiable relationship exists between, say, surface area and the number of structures present on a site, we can only alert the reader to the fact that our structural tallies in many instances are *minimum* figures. More comprehensive information will probably not be forthcoming until the sites have been excavated.

ARTIFACTUAL ANALYSIS

In order to ensure that the ceramic material gathered in the 1971 field survey would be entirely comparable with the excavated ceramics from the Arroyo Hondo site, we decided that the same person should analyze both collections. In addition to conducting a detailed examination of the freshly collected material (see Appendix C, p. 111), Richard W. Lang returned to the material from certain other sites in the study area that had been discovered and analyzed previously by the Laboratory of Anthropology. Unfortunately, this reexamination was not possible for all sites. Since, as has been noted previously, the ceramic type criteria of the northern Rio Grande are incompletely established and Lang's examination was perhaps more exacting than previous analyses (each sherd was examined under the binocular microscope for temper determination), our inability to return to all collections put us at a certain disadvantage when we attempted to classify and compare recorded sites in our survey area with those discovered in the 1971 season.

It is important to note in this connection that, because I was working alone in the field during most of the site survey, it was impossible for me to make systematic, intensive surface collections of the type described by Redman and Watson (1970) or Binford et al. (1970). Instead, surface collection had to be of the more traditional type in which the site was examined and artifactual material was collected without reference either to some scheme of rigid formal control or to statistical organization. The ceramic collections made at the various sites are thus not necessarily representative samples of the total ceramic universes present there. And the various percentages of ceramic types in these collections therefore do not *necessarily* represent the percentages of these types actually present at the various sites. The effect of this possible sampling error is to render dangerous any conclusions about the length or intensity of occupation of these sites based on these simple percentages.

Although the effects of sampling error of this kind cannot be completely eliminated in this analysis, an effort has been made to limit it by avoiding such conclusions on occupational intensity and the like. Instead, relying primarily on Breternitz's *An Appraisal of Tree-ring Dated Pottery in the Southwest* (1966), a time span or range of appearance and disappearance was assigned to each ceramic type present in the collections from each site. The occupation or occupations at that site were then assumed to have occurred sometime after the date of appearance of the earliest ceramic type but before the date of disappearance of the latest ceramic type represented in its surface collection. This simple application of *terminus a quo* and *terminus ad quem* reasoning produced a range

21

of years for each site during which, at some point, the site was presumed to have been used. This range of occupation was then translated into the northern Rio Grande period and phase system adopted for this study.

For example, the surface collection at site LA 8993 produced a number of ceramic types, the earliest of which is Socorro Black-on-white and the latest of which is Rio Grande Glaze I Yellow. According to Breternitz (1966:96,91), the best or most likely time span for the former type was between A.D. 1050 and about A.D. 1300 and for the latter type between about A.D. 1300 and A.D. 1450. Therefore, on the basis of the existing ceramic collections for LA 8993, we must conclude that the occupation probably occurred sometime between A.D. 1050 and A.D. 1450. Translated into our period and phase system (see p. 10), this means the site could have been occupied sometime between the Middle Phase of the Developmental Period and the Middle Phase of the Classic Period. Many sites, of course, may not actually have been occupied for the maximum time range possible.

Given the chronological aim of the survey and the existence in the northern Rio Grande of only the most rudimentary chronological frame for stone artifacts, we decided that limitations of time and money precluded a study of the survey lithic material. However, during the course of the survey, I attempted to collect all surface lithic material, including both tools and debitage.

THE SITE WEIGHT INDEX

This study sought to use the variations in site size and duration of occupation to learn something about the population history and carrying capacity of a specific region (see page 44). In order to obtain this kind of quantitative data, it is necessary to express the temporal and structural characteristics of the sites in numerical terms. One obvious means of doing this is simply to tally the number of sites in each area during each time period and then compare the totals. However, Gerkins, speaking of plant and animal ecology, points up the weakness of such an approach: "Total numbers are often not adequate to describe a population. Tree seedlings are obviously not equivalent to mature trees, and mosquito larvae living in a pond are not equivalent to mature insects. Weight is often a better expression than number, and population is called *biomass*" (1969:410).

In terms of archaeology, a 50-room pueblo occupied during two successive time periods is obviously not equivalent to a "field house" occupied during a similar time span. Yet conclusions about population fluctuations through time in a region made by simply comparing changes in the number of sites occupied during each period make just such an assumption of equivalency. However, the lack of archaeological data has led a number of scholars to use the "site" as this kind of single counter or basic unit for comparative purposes.

Perhaps the most successful study using this method was done by Schwartz (1956). Working in the Cohonina region of northeastern Arizona, Schwartz surveyed and dated over 100 Pueblo sites. He then divided the occupation span represented in the area into 25-year units and totaled the number of sites occupied during each of them. When these site totals were graphed unit by unit, they represented quantitatively what inferentially seemed to have been the population history of the area. That is, the period of initial settlement was one of low population density while the subsequent period witnessed a rapid population decline and the eventual abandonment of the area (Schwartz 1956:26–31). A more recent application of this technique may be found in Peckham and Wilson's (n.d.) unpublished survey of the Chuska Valley in New Mexico and Tuggle's (1970) work near the Mogollon Rim in Arizona.

Each of these studies provides an approximation of the actual prehistoric population curve in its area. However, the precision of such approximations is difficult to assess, since each study presents a site, be it large or small, simply as "a site," equal to 1 in the totals and represented as a unit equivalent to all other such units on the graphs.

A slightly different approach to this problem was made by John T. Hack (1942), who sought to reconstruct the population curve for the Jeddito Valley in northeastern Arizona as part of his physiographic study of the region. Like Schwartz, Tuggle, and Peckham and Wilson, Hack tallied sites by time periods and then graphed the results, but in addition he sought to correct for differences among sites by assigning them "units" based on their size and structural remains.

23

For example, a sherd area was assigned 2 units; a site with architectural remains was assigned 2 units for each structure. Anywhere from 2 to 70 additional units were added in proportion to the site's surface dimensions (1942:78). In this manner Hack obtained a corrected value for each of the sites in his survey area, which he then totaled by time periods and graphed to construct his relative population curve (1942:79).

Although this method takes site size differences into account, it has a weakness shared by the previously mentioned studies as well. That is, sites were very commonly occupied for more than one time period, making it necessary to count them more than once. Thus, using Hack's method, one would find that a site consisting of the remains of 20 structures occupied simultaneously during a 100-year period would have the same value in the population curve as a site consisting of 20 structures only 10 of which were ever occupied contemporaneously during the two 100-year periods of its occupation. Since the former site represents a greater population density than does the latter, assigning them both a value of 20 injects some distortion into the population curve. A more correct valuation of the sites would place them at 20 and 10, respectively.

Naturally, sites within our survey area varied in size and number of occupational phases. Given the objectives of the survey, therefore, we felt that a phase-by-phase tally of sites—even using Hack's method of adding values to sites in the total—would not provide sufficiently precise data. Ideally, what was needed was an accurate count of the actual number of structures at each site as well as a breakdown of those assignable to each phase. With this information we could assess the fluctuation in the occupation of each site through time. However, such information is often difficult to obtain even after excavation, and most of our site data had been obtained from surface examination only.

This problem—that is, the distortion inherent in a simple tally of raw site numbers for each phase, together with the impossibility of obtaining information on the actual proportion of structures in each phase at the various sites—led to our decision to assign each site in the survey area a numerical value, or weight, that expressed a relationship between the number (or estimated number) of structural units and the number of occupational phases found at each site. "Structural units" is here taken to mean inferred or observed archaeological remains that

24

suggest the former presence of a unit of construction occupied for domiciliary, ceremonial, storage, or other purposes. By "occupational phases" we are referring to the chronological framework adopted for this study. Basically, this framework consists of the time *periods* defined by Wendorf (1954) and the time *phases* defined both by Wetherington (1968) and the demands of our own data.

A simple procedure, the *site weight index*, was adopted to calculate the corrected value of sites used in this study. First, the number of occupational phases at a site was totaled, as was the number of structures recorded for it. The total number of structures was then divided by the total number of occupational phases and the product added to one. The resultant value was the *weight* of the site for each of its phases. For example, a site with four structures remaining on the surface that showed evidence of having been occupied for three temporal phases would be weighted as follows:

$$\frac{\text{total number of structures}}{\text{total number of phases}} + 1 = \text{site weight}$$

$$\frac{4}{3} + 1 = 2.33$$

This is the site's weight in each of the three phases during which it was occupied. The occupational density of settlement of the various areas during these three phases could then be compared with one another by totaling the weights of all the sites occupied during their respective time periods.

However, if the time phases are of different lengths, the effect of this difference on their site weights must be corrected in the following manner. The common denominator of the lengths of all phases is ascertained (in the middle northern Rio Grande this figure is 25). This common denominator is then divided into the lengths of all the phases and the quotients of these divisions are in turn divided into the site weight totals of each respective phase.

For example, the length of the Middle Phase of the Coalition Period is 50 years; the length of the Late or Galisteo Phase of the same period is 25 years. The difference in the length of these two time blocks makes it difficult for us to compare the relative magnitude of their settlement. That is, if the site weight total for the Middle Phase was greater than that of the Late Phase, we could not be sure that the difference was not simply due to the fact that the

25

former lasted longer than the latter. However, when we divide these two phases by the common denominator of all phases in the sequence, we obtain values (2 and 1, respectively, in the case of our example) that can then be divided into the total weight of the sites from each phase to correct for this difference. The resulting figure should be a close approximation of the true "weight" of settlement and population in each phase. In the case of our example, the gross site weight total for the Middle Phase is 433.17; for the Late Phase it is 863.70. When these figures are divided by 2 and 1, respectively, the resulting values are 216.59 and 863.70. These true or corrected weights can then be compared with one another without regard to differences in the temporal span of the phases to which they pertain.

If the entire site weighting procedure is a valid indicator of occupational density through time, then the phase with the higher corrected site weight total should have had the higher population density. Site weight totals may also be used to compare population histories in different geographical areas and to infer at least variations in human carrying capacity between them.[2]

I am aware of the possible distortions that might be introduced into a site's weight by the effects of such factors as differential preservation, the probability that only the latest structures in a multiphase site will survive to be counted, the possibility that not all temporal phases present on a site will be represented in the surface ceramics collections, and so forth. Use of the maximum possible time span for each site, combined with the likelihood that the actual number of structures present at many sites was often underestimated, renders our site weight totals very conservative. That is, it is likely that many sites were not actually occupied for the maximum time range we assigned to them and that thus the number of structures (which also may have been underestimated) was in some instances divided by too many phases. However, error thus introduced into our data base would tend to push our population curve downward and generally to smooth out variation within it. Since the population curve that has resulted from our site weight index totals exhibits rather dramatic changes despite this conservative bias, we have concluded that possible distortions from these sources do not represent a serious problem.

In general, the discounting of such possible distortions in the seriation and interpretation of site surface data is not without excellent precedent (cf. Phillips, Ford, and Griffin 1951:219–33; J. A. Ford 1949; for a more skeptical view see Rowe 1961:327). So, because *relative* data on population and human carrying capacity rather than *absolute* population figures are being sought, the error introduced into our data by these factors is presumed to be more or less uniform throughout our sample. It must be remembered, however, that such a presumption, together with the site weight index itself, is used strictly as a means of *approximating* quantified information that only large-scale excavation could, in fact, provide.

By means of this site weight index a weight, or value, was calculated for each site used in the study. These weights, together with the lifezone, temporal phases, number of structures, and natural district of each site, are presented in Table 5 (Appendix B). A summary of this information makes up the following chapter, after which the model of settlement pattern change is introduced and then used in an interpretation of Arroyo Hondo and northern Rio Grande prehistory.

3

Survey Results

The Arroyo Hondo site survey produced information on 65 previously unknown sites. We combined this information with the number of sites known from the sustaining area and with site data recorded earlier during the Cochiti Dam Archaeological Salvage Project and by the Museum of New Mexico Laboratory of Anthropology, bringing the total sample available for use in this study to 169. Although the survey was originally divided between the presumed sustaining area and the remainder of the transect, the purposes of this report do not call for such a division in presentation of the data. The following sections will summarize the results of the survey for the entire study area in terms of the nature, location, and chronological placement of recorded sites. In Appendix B, Table 5 presents basic information on each site, and Table 6 gives site components by period and phase. Unfortunately, limitations of space prevent the publication of full descriptions of the sites; these data are available in the survey field notes on file at the School of American Research and the Museum of New Mexico.

PRECERAMIC AND DEVELOPMENTAL PERIODS

Human exploitation of the study area appears to have begun in the Early or Preceramic Period of Rio Grande prehistory, extending from the late Pleistocene to about A.D. 600. Nine apparently Archaic chipping stations have been reported from the transect and a number of possibly Archaic lithic sites were encountered during the 1971 survey. These data will not be treated here, however, since the as yet unresolved problems of the Early Man and Archaic manifestations in the northern Rio Grande region are largely beyond the scope of this research.

Fully agricultural peoples apparently first settled in the survey area sometime after the beginning of the Early Phase of the Developmental Period around A.D. 600. Eleven sites are known from this phase, eight situated on the Rio Grande floodplain or terrace and three in the Santa Fe River Canyon area. Surface manifestations at these sites indicated they were small, isolated settlements, probably of low population. Five sites (LA 55, LA 177, LA 230, LA 6173, and LA 10686) consisted simply of scattered sherd and lithic debris. At three more sites, pithouse remains were discernible: six at LA 272, three at LA 6172, and one with a surface room at LA 6174. Site LA 249, a large site near the Rio Grande, seemed to have an Early Developmental ceramic component within an occupation apparently continuous until the Late Classic Period. Of the two remaining sites, LA 113 and LA 266, nothing beyond their sherd classes and locations was recorded in the Laboratory of Anthropology site files.

By the end of the Early Phase of the Developmental Period three sites were abandoned, while occupation continued at eight others, and 11 new sites were established. Thus, the number of sites in the survey area showed a net increase from 11 to 19 between the Early and Middle phases of the Developmental Period. This growth was not uniform throughout the transect; 18 sites remained concentrated in the vicinity of the Rio Grande floodplain and terraces and in the Santa Fe River Canyon. Only one site (LA 10609) probably dating to the Middle Phase of the Developmental Period was encountered outside these two river valleys in the Arroyo Hondo Pueblo sustaining area.

Surface manifestations at the 19 Middle Phase sites varied considerably. Five sites (LA 55, LA 230, LA 256, LA 10684, and LA 10686) were simply sherd and lithic scatters. Sites LA 113, LA 266, and LA 150 had no structural information recorded in the Laboratory of Anthropology site files. Of the remaining 11, two sites (LA 272 and LA 6174) included one or more pithouses. At a third site (LA 10609), structures from a Historic reoccupation may have obscured most surface manifestations dating to the Developmental Period, but a circular depression near the remains of one of the later buildings suggested a subsurface structure such as a pithouse. The additional eight sites (LA 247, LA 249, LA 328, LA 329, LA 331, LA 332, LA 10678, and LA 10692) all exhibited contiguous-walled pueblo ruins.

It should be noted that two of the three pithouse sites (LA 272 and LA 6174) included an Early as well as a Middle Developmental component. In contrast, only one of the Middle Phase surface pueblos (LA 249) showed evidence of an Early Phase occupation as well. Thus, the pithouse sites appear to fall at the early end of the Middle Phase and the pueblos at the later end. This pattern tends to support Wendorf's assertion that the later portion of the Developmental Period witnessed a transition in domestic architecture from the subsurface pithouse to the surface, contiguous-walled pueblo (1954:206).

By the end of the Middle Phase of the Developmental Period, 10 of the 19 sites previously occupied in the transect were abandoned. Occupation apparently continued into the subsequent Late or Tesuque Phase at the remaining sites, and 15 new ones were established, resulting in a net increase from 19 to 25 sites from the Middle through the Late Phase of the Developmental Period.

Of the 14 new sites in the transect, only three were located outside the Santa Fe River Canyon and the Rio Grande floodplain and terraces. Of these, La 10621 lay east of the Rio Grande in Tetilla Canyon on the western edge of La Bajada Mesa, and LA 191 and LA 10614 were found in the sustaining area of Arroyo Hondo Pueblo. These site locations seem to indicate a trend toward expansion of settlement outside the major river valleys in the survey area during the Late Phase of the Developmental Period.

Surface manifestations at Late Phase sites included three sherd scatters (LA 256, LA 10654, LA 10686) and one site (LA 150) for which no structural information was recorded. Of the 21 Late Phase sites for which structural information exists, 18 contained the remains of contiguous-walled pueblos. Site LA 10621 was a rockshelter, and the three remaining sites consisted of pithouses. These included LA 9140, with three such structures; LA 191, with four to six pithouses associated with the charred remains of an undetermined number of jacal surface structures; and LA 10614, with a single pithouse depression near a small masonry surface room. These pithouse sites are interesting exceptions to the trend toward surface domiciliary structures at this time.

By the end of the Development Period, 13 of the 25 sites previ-

31

ously occupied in the study area were abandoned. Occupation apparently continued at 12 sites, while 17 new settlements were established, to produce net growth from 25 to 29 sites by the Early Phase of the Coalition Period.

COALITION PERIOD

Of the Early Coalition sites, 26 were located in either the Santa Fe River Canyon or the Rio Grande floodplain and terrace areas. In addition, site LA 10621, the rock-shelter site in Tetilla Canyon, remained occupied during this phase, and two sites (LA 76 and LA 10701) appeared in the Arroyo Hondo sustaining area. Thus it seems that the trend toward settlement outside the major river valleys continued in the study area during the Early Coalition Period.

Surface manifestations at Early Phase sites included a single sherd scatter (LA 265) and four other sites (LA 113, LA 150, LA 266, and LA 333) for which no structural data were recorded at the Laboratory of Anthropology. Site LA 10701, in the sustaining area, consisted of a possible subsurface structure indicated by a soil stain and a few sherds in a recent foundation trench. The remaining 23 sites can be classed as contiguous-walled pueblos ranging from fewer than 10 structural units with no kivas to roughly 500 units with four kivas (LA 7). Included in this range is the single, large Early Coalition site in the sustaining area, LA 76, where 45 to 50 rooms were arranged in a U-shaped mound around a central plaza containing a possible kiva depression. With over 1,000 units, another site, LA 16, exceeded even the preceding size range, although its Early Coalition component was only one in a multicomponent occupation.

The wide range in site size during the Early Phase of the Coalition Period, along with the presence of several exceptionally large sites, is especially significant when it is noted that the largest site exhibiting Developmental Period ceramic material had around 200 units and that the largest strictly Developmental Period site (LA 166) comprised between 50 and 75 units. It seems clear that an increase in site size as well as numbers took place in the survey area during the Early Phase of the Coalition Period.

By the beginning of the Middle Phase of the Coalition Period, four of the 29 sites previously occupied in the study area were abandoned. Occupation apparently continued at the remaining 25 sites, and four new ones appeared, resulting in no net change in the number of sites between the first two phases of the Coalition Period.

All Middle Coalition sites outside the Arroyo Hondo sustaining area were located in the Santa Fe River Canyon or on the Rio Grande floodplain and terraces. In the sustaining area, however, not only did settlement continue at LA 76 but the major occupation there probably took place. Thus, there seems to have been no decline in population outside the two riverine areas, and perhaps even some settlement growth instead.

Surface manifestations at Middle Coalition sites included four sherd scatters (LA 265, LA 369, LA 408, and LA 409) and four sites (LA 149, LA 150, LA 265, and LA 266) for which no structural information has been recorded. With the possible exception of the poorly known pithouse site (LA 10701) mentioned earlier, the remaining sites were surface pueblo remains ranging from two to approximately 1,000 rooms. Some of these large pueblos span more than one phase of the chronological sequence.

By the end of the Middle Phase of the Coalition Period, 11 of the 29 sites previously occupied in the survey area were abandoned, while occupation apparently continued into the following Late or Galisteo Phase at the remaining 18 sites. In addition, six new sites were established, resulting in a net decrease from 29 to 24 sites.

As in the preceding phase, all sites known from the Late Coalition were located in the Santa Fe River Canyon, on the Rio Grande floodplain and terraces, or in the Arroyo Hondo sustaining area. The last area held only two of the 24 known sites, but one of these was Arroyo Hondo Pueblo itself, founded about A.D. 1300. Site LA 76, the second one, overlapped partially with Arroyo Hondo Pueblo but was probably abandoned before the end of the Late Coalition Period. Perhaps the inhabitants of LA 76 were absorbed into the population of the neighboring site downstream. Whatever the case, Arroyo Hondo Pueblo experienced its greatest period of growth at about this time.

Surface manifestations at sites of the Late Phase of the Coalition Period included three sherd scatters (LA 369, LA 408, and LA 409) and three sites for which no structural information has been recorded (LA 149, LA 150, and LA 266). The remaining 18 sites were all pueblo ruins that, on the basis of surface inspection, exhibited the same range in numbers of structural units as found in sites of the preceding Middle Phase.

CLASSIC PERIOD

By the end of the Coalition Period, nine of the 24 sites previously occupied in the study area were abandoned. Occupation apparently continued into the following Early Phase of the Classic Period at the
remaining 15 sites, while 14 new ones appeared, resulting in a net increase from 24 to 29 sites between the Late Phase of the Coalition and
the Early Phase of the Classic Period. This site total is equal to the high
achieved during the Early and Middle phases of the Coalition Period.

Of the 14 new sites in the survey area, six were located outside
the Santa Fe River Canyon and Rio Grande floodplain and terrace
areas. One of these sites, LA 10655, was a sherd and lithic scatter
located near an arroyo canyon on top of La Bajada Mesa east of the
Rio Grande. Three sites located in Tetilla Canyon were LA 10617, a
fieldhouse; LA 10625, a sherd and lithic scatter; and LA 10621, the
Developmental Period rock-shelter that shows evidence of reoccupation at this time. In the sustaining area, two minor sites appeared
during the Early Classic. Site LA 10612 consisted of a sherd scatter,
a boulder circle, and some possible agricultural terraces; and LA
10700 was a single, partially restorable vessel dating to either the
Early or Middle Phase of the Classic Period. In terms strictly of site
numbers, then, the Early Classic Period seems to have been a time
of settlement expansion outside the riverine areas of the study area.

Surface manifestations at the remaining Early Phase sites included
two shrines, LA 6295 and LA 8720, while one site (LA 149) had no structural information on record. The additional 20 sites exhibited the same
range in numbers of structural units as those of the Coalition Period,
but there appeared to be a greater percentage of smaller ruins at this
time. Arroyo Hondo Pueblo underwent a virtual abandonment during
this phase, followed by reoccupation at a much lower population level.

By the end of the Early Phase of the Classic Period at least eight of
the 29 sites previously occupied in the transect were abandoned. Occupation apparently continued into the subsequent Middle Phase of
the Classic Period at the remaining 21 sites, and three new sites became established, resulting in another net decrease from 29 to 24 sites.
Of the three new sites, only one (LA 5) lay outside the Rio Grande and
Santa Fe River subareas, but this was a major site consisting of 166 or
more structures located on the flats above Tetilla Canyon. In addition,
occupation apparently continued into this phase at the three earlier

sites in the vicinity of Tetilla Canyon (LA 10617, LA 10621, and LA 10625), and at site LA 10655 on La Bajada Mesa. Early in the Middle Classic Period, however, Arroyo Hondo Pueblo was abandoned permanently and the sustaining area virtually emptied.

Surface manifestations at the sites of the Middle Phase of the Classic Period included two sherd scatters (LA 10625 and LA 10655), two rock-shelter sites (LA 4445 and LA 10621), and two shrines (LA 6295 and LA 8720). The possible agricultural terrace site in the sustaining area (LA 10612) may date to this period as well. The remaining 17 sites were all pueblo ruins of the same size range noted previously for the Early Classic and Coalition periods.

By the end of the Middle Phase of the Classic Period, 16 of the 24 sites previously occupied in the transect were abandoned. Occupation apparently continued into the subsequent Late Phase at the remaining eight sites, and one new site became established, resulting in a dramatic drop in the number of sites occupied from 23 to nine.

All sites of the Late Phase of the Classic Period were located exclusively in the two riverine subareas of the transect. The Arroyo Hondo sustaining area was apparently uninhabited during this phase. Surface manifestations at the nine dated sites included one rock-shelter site, LA 4445; one shrine, LA 6295; and one site, LA 165, for which no structural data had been recorded. The remaining six sites all contained pueblo ruins, but the range in number of structures was greatly reduced from that of the preceding phases. Abandonment of the 1,000-room site, LA 16, made site LA 7, with only half as many structures, the largest site in the study area. Four sites (LA 70, LA 126, LA 249, and LA 6455) exhibited between 100 and 200 structures each, and a fifth Late Phase pueblo (LA 6460) had only four to six structures recorded.

HISTORIC PERIOD

By the end of the Classic Period, six of the nine sites previously occupied were abandoned, including most of the pueblos and the only shrine dating to the Late Classic Period. Occupation apparently continued into the Historic Period at one of the pueblos (LA 126), at the rock-shelter site (LA 4445), and at the undescribed site (LA 165). At the same time, 35 sites came into existence and eight were reoccupied, resulting in a net increase from nine to 46 sites between the

Classic and Historic periods. Of these 46 sites, nine were located outside the Rio Grande and Santa Fe River subareas. In the vicinity of Tetilla Canyon, LA 10624, LA 10626, and LA 10628 were found, and on the edge of La Bajada Mesa, LA 10659. At least five sites are known from the Historic Period in the sustaining area. Structural remains were fewer at these Historic sites than during the Pueblo occupation, suggesting ranchitos and homesteads rather than small communities.

Finally, it should be mentioned that four sites located in the sustaining area proved undatable for a variety of reasons. Site LA 10608 is a circular pile of rocks on a hilltop 0.4 mile southeast of Arroyo Hondo Pueblo. Its shape and location suggest that the site was a shrine, probably associated with the main pueblo's occupation. Site LA 10610 is a possible agricultural field house in Arroyo Hondo Canyon about 0.1 mile downstream from the pueblo. Sites LA 10613 and LA 10615, on the western and eastern margins of the sustaining area, respectively, consist simply of a few rock wall outlines.

POPULATION HISTORY OF THE STUDY AREA

Settlement in the study area certainly began in the Early Period before A.D. 600. Exploitation of the area by fully agricultural peoples very likely began sometime after that date, initiating the Early Phase of the Developmental Period. Whether this new adaptation was undertaken by immigrants or indigenous peoples cannot be determined from present evidence. Whoever these people were, the limited scale of their initial occupation is attested by the small number of sites known in the transect from this Early Phase. Further, the low value of the corrected site weight for this time block (Tables 1–3) appears to indicate that these sites were small and supported a very low population. However, we have clear evidence of the success of this agricultural adaptation in the two subsequent phases of the Developmental Period. Between the Early and Middle phases of that period, the number of sites in the transect increased by one-half, while their corrected site weight total grew fourfold (Fig. 2). Between the Middle and Late phases of the Developmental Period the number of sites increased by slightly less than one-third, and the corrected site weight again grew to four times its former level. Between the Early and the Late phases, the gross number of sites doubled, but the corrected site weight total is 16 times greater than the

TABLE 1.
Cultural Sequence and Site Weight Totals in the Study Area (Transect and Sustaining Area)

Period and Phase	Number of Sites Occupied in Phase	Gross Site Weight Total	Divisor [a]	Corrected Site Weight Total
Developmental Period				
Early Phase	11	36.88	12	3.07
Middle Phase	19	96.43	8	12.05
Late Phase	25	204.02	4	51.01
Coalition Period				
Early Phase	29	563.92	2	281.96
Middle Phase	30	433.17	2	216.59
Late Phase	25	863.70	1	863.70
Classic Period				
Early Phase	30	869.04	3	289.68
Middle Phase	25	1008.44	4	252.11
Late Phase	9	170.37	4	42.59
Historic Period	46	252.11	12	21.01

[a]The "divisor" is the number that results when the length of the phase in years is divided by the common denominator of the length of each phase. This figure is then divided into the *gross* site weight total for the phase to obtain the *corrected* site weight total.

37

TABLE 2.
Cultural Sequence and Site Weight Totals in the Arroyo Hondo Pueblo Sustaining Area

Period and Phase	Number of Sites Occupied in Phase	Gross Site Weight Total	Divisor [a]	Corrected Site Weight Total
Developmental Period				
Early Phase	—	—	12	—
Middle Phase	1	1.50	8	0.19
Late Phase	2	8.00	4	2.00
Coalition Period				
Early Phase	2	14.25	2	7.13
Middle Phase	2	14.25	2	7.13
Late Phase	2	513.91	1	513.91
Classic Period				
Early Phase	3	504.16	3	168.05
Middle Phase	2	503.16	4	125.79
Late Phase	—	—	4	—
Historic	5	6.50	12	0.54

[a]The "divisor" is the number that results when the length of the phase in years is divided by the common denominator of the length of each phase. This figure is then divided into the *gross* site weight total for the phase to obtain the *corrected* site weight total.

TABLE 3.
Cultural Sequence and Site Weight Totals in the Survey Transect

Period and Phase	Number of Sites Occupied in Phase	Gross Site Weight Total	Divisor[a]	Corrected Site Weight Total
Developmental Period				
Early Phase	11	36.88	12	3.07
Middle Phase	18	94.93	8	11.87
Late Phase	23	196.02	4	49.01
Coalition Period				
Early Phase	27	549.67	2	274.84
Middle Phase	28	418.92	2	209.46
Late Phase	23	349.79	1	349.79
Classic Period				
Early Phase	27	364.88	3	121.63
Middle Phase	23	505.28	4	126.32
Late Phase	9	170.37	4	42.59
Historic Period	41	245.61	12	20.47

[a]The "divisor" is the number that results when the length of the phase in years is divided by the common denominator of the length of each phase. This figure is then divided into the *gross* site weight total for the phase to obtain the *corrected* site weight total.

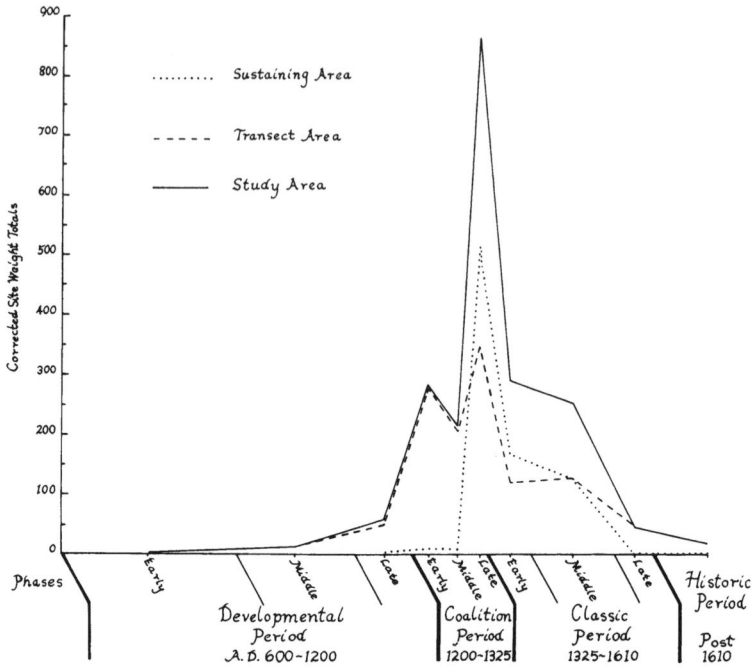

FIG. 2.   Relative Population Magnitudes through Time in the Transect, Sustaining Area, and Study Area

early level. If our site weight calculation can be relied upon, this may be taken as evidence of steady and highly dynamic population growth throughout the 600 years of the Developmental Period, resulting in its final phase in the expansion of settlement outside the main riverine heartland of the transect.

While these apparent increases in site number, site size, and population density are quite marked during the Developmental Period, they do not seem to be outside the range of population growth and expansion to be expected from a small, successful human population exploiting a new environment or possesed of a new means of coping with an old one. Further, at this early stage of technical development in Pueblo agriculture, it is possible that at least some of the increase in the numbers of sites in the first two phases of the Developmental Period is partly a reflection of seasonal residence changes made by the same groups rather than additional autonomous habitation units made by more people.

A clearer increase in the density of population in the transect occurred with the onset of the subsequent Coalition Period. During the Early Phase of that period the corrected site weight increased to a level 5½ times greater than that of the final phase of the Developmental Period. However, at the same time the number of sites in the study area increased by only about one-sixth, that is, by four sites. Unlike the growth during the Developmental Period, the settlement changes in the Early Phase of the Coalition Period cannot be interpreted as largely due to a proliferation of seasonally occupied sites of a stable or only gradually expanding population. This is, of course, because the geometric change in site weight values can be ascribed to growth (or perhaps "coalescence") within existing sites rather than to a great increase in the total number of sites. Interestingly, despite this apparent increase in population density, no corresponding major expansion from the two main drainages into other areas of the transect occurred during this Early Phase. Also, site numbers and site weight totals remained essentially unchanged in the sustaining area at this time and did not experience a similar period of growth until the Late Phase of the Coalition Period.

While population growth on a large scale certainly occurred during the first part of the Coalition Period, the source of that growth remains elusive. The magnitude of the change seems too large to have been generated solely within the local population. That local growth was supplemented by immigrants from outside the transect seems possible and even likely, but who they were and where they came from have yet to be determined.

During the subsequent Middle Phase of the Coalition Period a rather unexpected decline in the corrected site weight totals occurred, although the number of sites in the study area remained nearly constant. It would appear that some reversal occurred in the long-term trend toward population growth and coalescence.

The last phase of the Coalition Period apparently witnessed a reversal in the decline in population density in the study area, but this reversal is reflected in our indices in an odd manner. While the total number of sites occupied in the transect declined by one-sixth between the Middle and Late phases, the corrected site weight total increased by a factor of four. Most of this growth was due to the founding of Arroyo Hondo Pueblo and its rapid population increase between about A.D. 1300 and A.D. 1330. Still, corrected site weight

41

totals for the remainder of the study area rose by about two-thirds between the Middle and Late Coalition.

In the Early Phase of the Classic Period, the gross number of sites in the survey area increased by one-sixth. Despite this, the population density, as measured by the corrected site weight totals, sank sharply to one-third the level of the Late Phase of the Coalition Period. The decline at Arroyo Hondo alone was of even greater magnitude. Whether this decline in our indices indicates a disastrous series of events, such as famine with its high mortality and migration, cannot be determined by present evidence. The most widely accepted explanation, that climatic oscillations and concomitant crop failures are at the heart of the matter, is discussed in Chapter 4. It is especially surprising, in light of this decline, that four of the new sites recorded for the transect are outside the two main riverine areas and in the vicinity of Tetilla Canyon.

The following Middle Phase of the Classic Period witnessed a very slight downward movement in the corrected site weight total, and the gross number of sites in the study area dropped by one-sixth. Most of the site weight decrease, however, was due to the abandonment of Arroyo Hondo Pueblo; in the remainder of the study area the index remained virtually constant. Whatever the cause of this apparent stabilization of population in the study area, it was fairly short-lived. During the Late Phase of the Classic Period the number of sites dropped to about two-thirds their Middle Phase level, and the corrected site weight total again dropped to roughly one-sixth the previous level. Two factors presumably related to this decline are the apparent climatic deteriorations noted in the tree-ring records for the sixteenth century (Smiley, Stubbs, and Bannister 1953:51; Fritts 1965) and the possibility that Old World epidemic diseases reached the Southwest in advance of actual European contact and colonization, as they apparently did in the Caddoan areas of the central Mississippi valley during the seventeenth century (Sears 1964:283).

4

The Model of Settlement Pattern Change

As mentioned earlier, the hypothetical model generated prior to the site survey project (Dickson 1975) was not supported by the data; instead, an alternative model that better described the data emerged. We had expected that one area of the transect would hold the early sites and lack the late ones. The observed pattern, however, was that sites clustered in six concentrations and that two of these clusters included both the earliest and the latest sites encountered. Upon examination of the physical surroundings of these site clusters, it became apparent that the six areas could be defined by the presence of certain combinations of exploitable resources. These areas are here termed *natural districts* and are central to the model to be presented in this chapter.

DEFINITION AND DESCRIPTION OF NATURAL DISTRICTS

"Natural district" denotes a special kind of geographical subarea of a given region, one whose physical properties and exploitable natural resources render it different in a qualitative way from other subareas in its capacity to support or "carry" human populations. The physical properties that seem most salient in distinguishing the natural districts of the Pueblo cultures of the middle northern Rio

Grande region include (1) nature and amount of available water, (2) types of natural lifezones, and (3) physiographic features or land-forms.

According to Nietschmann, human carrying capacity refers to "the theoretical maximum population total at a subsistence level which can be supported with a given technology without environmental degradation. The concept implies a measurable equilibrium relationship between population resources and environmental quality" (1972:63).

However, as Nietschmann further notes, carrying capacity formulas have been difficult to apply to the study of human ecology due to "conceptual as well as data acquisition problems" (1972:63). While he is referring to the problems of studying the carrying capacity of the environments of living groups, his remark would seem even more germane to attempts to assess carrying capacity of the environments of peoples known only archaeologically. No claim is made that problems inherent in assessing carrying capacity in archaeology have been solved, but it does appear that the site weight index offers a simple means of comparing the size and duration of human settlement between natural districts and that using the results of this calculation, the relative differences in human carrying capacity between natural districts can be estimated.

We assumed that in a given region, the distribution of resources is a primary factor in determining the distribution of human settlement. We further assumed that when a region is subdivided into subareas or natural districts in terms of the variations in the distribution of these natural resources, the size and duration of the human settlements within these districts will reflect this resource variation. Therefore, by calculating the weights of sites in terms of their size and duration of settlement and then totaling these site weights phase by phase for each natural district, we have a rough means of comparing the human carrying capacity of each natural district through time. Of course, even though natural districts are determined largely with reference to their physical or natural properties, the distributions of the human settlements within them can be predicted and their human carrying capacity accounted for only when the socio-cultural attributes (for example, technical level, economic integration, and specific history) of their human occupants are taken into consideration.

44

It should be noted that the natural districts discussed in this report were first recognized and defined using differences in the history and magnitude of their human occupation, but we inferred that these differences were largely reflections of variations in certain natural resources from district to district. In other words, although we use natural resources more or less exclusively to define our natural districts in the following section, this is clearly a *post hoc* effort. In the future, however, it should be possible to define such districts and to rank them according to their human carrying capacity, in *advance* of field survey, strictly by reference to selected natural criteria. Following such a site survey, it would be possible to check the advance district definitions against the site locations actually observed in the field.

Through analysis of the 1971 survey data, seven natural districts were recognized within the study area (Map 3). These were ranked relative to one another and then classified as possessing primary, secondary, tertiary, marginal, or submarginal suitability for human use on the basis of the magnitude of settlement that each supported through time, as indicated by their site weight index totals (Table 4). That is, the districts producing the highest site weight totals were classed as being of primary resource potential, those with the second highest totals as secondary, and so forth. The classification was as follows.

Primary
1. The Rio Grande floodplain and terraces south of the mouth of White Rock Canyon
2. Santa Fe River Canyon

Secondary
3. Upper Arroyo Hondo Canyon and the western foothills of the Sangre de Cristo Mountains
4. Tetilla Canyon

Tertiary
5. The middle Arroyo Hondo drainage

Marginal
6. The unnamed canyon on the western edge of La Bajada Mesa

Submarginal
7. The remaining intervening areas of the study area

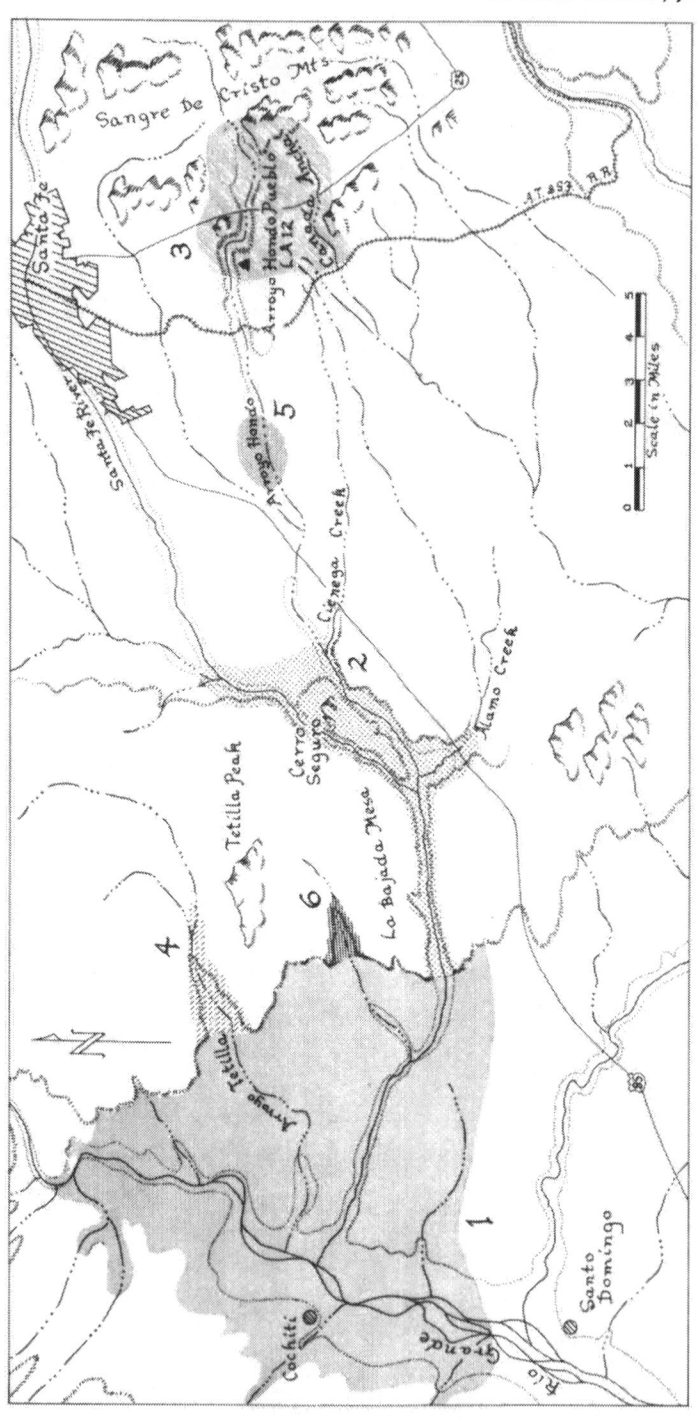

MAP 3. The Natural Districts Recognized in the Study Area

TABLE 4.
Cultural Sequence and Site Weight Totals in the Six Natural Districts in the Study Area.

Period and Phase	Number of Sites Occupied During Phase in Each Natural District							Corrected Site Weight Total by Phase in Each Natural District						
	1	2	3	4	5	6	Total	1	2	3	4	5	6	Total
Developmental Period														
Early Phase	8	3	0	0	0	0	11	2.82	.25	0	0	0	0	3.07
Middle Phase	11	7	1	0	0	0	19	10.37	1.50	.19	0	0	0	12.06*
Late Phase	11	11	0	1	2	0	25	30.11	18.46	0	.44	2.00	0	51.01
Coalition Period														
Early Phase	20	6	2	1	0	0	29	100.04	173.92	7.13	.88	0	0	281.97*
Middle Phase	23	5	3	0	0	0	31	106.04	103.42	7.13	0	0	0	216.59
Late Phase	17	6	2	0	0	0	25	141.95	207.84	513.91	0	0	0	863.70
Classic Period														
Early Phase	12	11	3	3	0	1	30	47.38	72.50	168.05	1.42	0	.33	289.68
Middle Phase	7	11	1	4	0	1	24	28.63	54.63	125.79	42.81	0	.25	252.11
Late Phase	5	4	0	0	0	0	9	22.55	20.04	0	0	0	0	42.59
Historic Period	14	23	5	3	0	1	46	5.15	13.90	.54	1.08	0	.33	21.00*

*The slight deviation of this figure from the total presented in Table 1 results from separate calculation of the natural district site weight totals and the rounding off of these totals to the second decimal place. It does not indicate a lack of correspondence between the two figures.

In our study area, the single most important factor differentiating the natural districts appeared to be the nature of their water supply. However, recall that in our survey design we divided the area into quarter sections, classified these units into one of three groups based on the kinds of water available within them, and then selected an unequal sample from each class for field surveying. Thus, since we had initially stratified our sample this way, the importance of water in differentiating our natural districts might conceivably be an artifact of our sampling design. In light of the strength of correlation between settlement and water supply, however, the probability of this seems low. In any case, the nature of the water supply in our natural districts can be summarized as follows:

Primary
> Rainfall and intermittent runoff
> Perennial springs
> Perennial streamflow
> More than 100 acres of arable land

Secondary
> Rainfall and intermittent runoff
> Perennial springs
> 50 to 100 acres of arable land

Tertiary
> Rainfall and intermittent runoff
> 10 to 50 acres of arable land

Marginal and submarginal
> Rainfall and intermittent runoff
> Less than 10 acres of arable land

These criteria only generally characterize the natural districts in the study area; a more detailed discussion of the seven districts follows.

1. The Rio Grande Floodplain and Terraces

This natural district fills the entire western third of the study area. It extends north as far as an imaginary line drawn perpendicular to the Rio Grande just below its debouchment from White Rock Canyon and south to an imaginary line drawn between Santo Domingo Canyon on the west to the south side of the mouth of the Santa Fe River Canyon. The western boundary is the second Pleistocene terrace west of the Rio Grande, and its eastern boundary is the edge of La Bajada Mesa. The physiography of the province can be divided into three separate zones:

1. The Rio Grande floodplain (Fig. 3), which ranges from 0.75 to 2 miles in width about 5,200 feet above sea level and contains perennially flowing water.
2. The eastern terraces of the Rio Grande, which slope gently downward from the foot of the cliffs of La Bajada Mesa at an elevation of about 5,600 feet to the edge of the modern river floodplain at about 5,200 feet. The descent is broken slightly by two highly dissected major river terraces 100 and 200 feet, respectively, above the modern floodplain. These flats are more or less perpendicular to the meandering beds of the Santa Fe River and several other lesser tributaries of the Rio Grande.
3. The western terraces of the Rio Grande, which slope downward more abruptly from the edge of the Rio Grande Canyon than do those on the east. These terraces on the west are also narrower and less dissected by erosion than their eastern counterparts.

Four biological lifezones characterize this natural province. The eastern flats are essentially shortgrass plains with scattered juniper trees, which increase in number in areas with slightly higher moisture. Although the Santa Fe River crosses these flats underground, at one point it surfaces to form a permanent seep known as Cochiti Springs; at these springs elements of the riparian lifezone occur. The Rio Grande floodplain supports essentially two zones: a riparian assemblage along the river channel and a shortgrass plains lifezone over the remainder of its area. The western terraces begin with a shortgrass plains assemblage nearest the river and then move, with increasing altitude, through juniper–shortgrass plains into a thin piñon-juniper assemblage.

Within the study area, the agricultural potential of this natural

49

FIG. 3. Natural District 1: The Rio Grande Floodplain and Terraces near Cochiti Pueblo

district seems to be matched only by that of the Santa Fe River Canyon. Arable land is concentrated in the following locations (in order of descending importance): (1) the floodplain of the Rio Grande; (2) the floodplains of its tributaries, including the Santa Fe River; (3) the arroyo canyons that dissect the terraces; and (4) the flats between the terrace edges.

The primacy of the first district, the Rio Grande floodplain, is probably based on a number of factors; major considerations certainly include the perennially available water of the river itself, the relative ease with which this water can be diverted for irrigation purposes, the renewal and fertilization of the soil on the plain through seasonal flooding by the river, and the ample amount of tillable land. Presumably, the tributary arroyos and stream beds were less attractive than the floodplain of the main river, but based on the number of sites located along or near them, it seems clear that they were heavily used as well. Although today these streams contain surface flow only intermittently, this was not necessarily the case in the past. Further, the smaller volume of their flow compared to that of the main river may have made fields planted on their floodplains somewhat less vulnerable to destruction by washout.

There is no direct evidence on record that either the arroyo canyons on the terrace edges or the flats between the terraces were farmed prehistorically. The use of the arroyos is suggested as likely on the basis of the ethnographic example of the Hopi and other southwestern Indian groups (Hack 1942:30–31). Planting on the flats would probably have required either a slightly greater rainfall regime than currently holds in the area or the use of water diversion techniques of some kind. In light of the abundantly available arable land in the immediate vicinity of the Rio Grande and its tributaries, however, it seems likely that if either the arroyos or the flats were farmed, it was done as a backup to the main efforts on the perennially watered land.

The cultural history of this natural district, together with that of the Santa Fe River Canyon, has already been discussed. Suffice it to say that the entire cultural sequence in the middle northern Rio Grande is represented here and that it has the second highest total number of sites (61) recorded for it and the second largest phase-by-phase site weight totals after the Santa Fe River Canyon (see Table 4).

2. The Santa Fe River Canyon

This natural district is located approximately in the middle of the survey transect and is largely coterminous with the course of the Santa Fe River and some of its major tributaries (Fig. 4). The western boundary of the district is the mouth of the Santa Fe River Canyon at the point where it debouches onto the eastern terraces of the Rio Grande. The northern boundary is the top edge of the Santa Fe River Canyon along the edge of La Bajada Mesa. The southern boundary of the province is defined by the southern edge of the canyon and the course of Alamo Creek, a major tributary of the Santa Fe River. The eastern boundary is formed by an irregular line traced north from Cerro de la Cruz along Cienega Creek to its junction with Arroyo Hondo. Both of these streams are tributaries of the Santa Fe River.

FIG. 4.   Natural District 2: The Santa Fe River Canyon

52

Physiographically, this natural district consists of four main zones: (1) the banks and floodplains of the Santa Fe River and its tributaries; (2) the terraces flanking the Santa Fe River and its tributaries; (3) the walls and side canyons of the Santa Fe River Canyon; and (4) the hilly plateau area on which Cerro Seguro is located above the junction of the Santa Fe River and its major tributaries.

Two main biological lifezones are found in this natural district. The floodplains and banks of the Santa Fe River and its tributaries that contain perennial water support a riparian lifezone. The terraces of the perennially flowing streams and the banks, floodplains, and terraces of the intermittently flowing ones support a shortgrass plains lifezone. Junipers occur in this shortgrass plains setting in densities that vary depending on available moisture. The walls and side canyons also support a shortgrass plains lifezone and scattered junipers, which tend to have a greater density on somewhat moister north-facing slopes. The hilly plateau area above the river junctions supports the heaviest growth of junipers in the natural district, and its lifezone perhaps deserves the designation juniper-shortgrass plains.

Arable land seems to be concentrated in the following locations (in order of descending importance): (1) the floodplains of the Santa Fe River and its tributaries; (2) the terraces of the Santa Fe River and its *perennially* flowing tributaries; (3) the larger side canyons of the Santa Fe River Canyon; (4) the flats on the plateau south of Cerro Seguro; and (5) the arroyos draining the plateau north of Cerro Seguro.

As in the case of the Rio Grande natural district, and for essentially the same reasons, the floodplains in this district seem to offer the greatest agricultural potential. The only real disadvantage of floodplain farming would, of course, be the danger of crop washout due to heavy flooding. As a means of ensuring a crop in the event of such flooding, it is likely that the terraces surrounding the floodplains, together with the side canyon arroyos, were also farmed. While the flats on the plateau above the canyon could not support crops at present, they are sufficiently rich in nutrients that given greater rainfall, they could be dry farmed (N. Edmund Kelley: personal communication). Whether or not such farming was ever practiced there is difficult to say. A major site, LA 3, is located on these flats, but given the abundance of water in the canyon below, it is very likely that the fields associated

53

with this site were there. Finally, the arroyos north of Cerro Seguro might lend themselves to exploitation in the manner described for the Hopi by Hack (1942), but the soil is extremely thin
and rocky, rendering such use rather unlikely.

Seventy sites are recorded for the Santa Fe River district, more
than in any other natural district in the study area. However, a survey of the Rio Grande natural district as intense as the one done in
1971 in the Santa Fe River Canyon would probably reveal an even
greater number of sites in the former area. This surmise is based on
the potential of the abundant acreage in the Rio Grande floodplain
for the support of a larger population than that of the more limited
floodplain and terrace acreage in the narrow canyon of the Santa Fe
River. In any case, the entire middle northern Rio Grande cultural
sequence is represented in the Santa Fe River Canyon natural district, and on the basis of the site weight totals, population densities
here were consistently as great or greater than in any other district
in the transect.

3. The Upper Arroyo Hondo Canyon and the Western Foothills of the Sangre de Cristo Mountains

This natural district, located on the far eastern edge of the study
area, makes up the bulk of the Arroyo Hondo Pueblo sustaining
area. It is centered on the upper canyon of the Arroyo Hondo in
that section of its length that passes through the first three roughly
parallel rows of foothills of the Sangre de Cristo Mountain chain.
The west-running Arroyo Hondo Canyon cuts through these rows of
hills at a generally perpendicular angle (Fig. 5).

The western boundary of this natural district is an imaginary line
drawn perpendicular to Arroyo Hondo Canyon and running parallel
to and about one-half mile west of the westernmost row of foothills
of the Sangre de Cristos. The northern and southern boundaries are
located within the foothills between 0.5 and 0.75 mile on either side
of the arroyo canyon.

The physiography of the district includes three zones: (1) the
floodplain and terraces of the Arroyo Hondo, (2) the gently rolling
piedmont at the edge of the Arroyo Hondo Canyon and the foot of
the westernmost row of foothills of the Sangre de Cristo Mountains,
and (3) the foothills of the Sangre de Cristo Mountains.

FIG. 5.   Natural District 3: Upper Arroyo Hondo Canyon and the Western Foothills of the Sangre de Cristo Mountains

Four biological lifezones characterize this natural district. The canyon bottom, at various points along its length where springs or seeps make water perennially available, supports a riparian lifezone. Elsewhere in the canyon, water is only intermittently available in the form of runoff and rainfall; here the lifezone is generally piñon and juniper trees on the banks and terraces of the arroyo and various herbaceous species associated with the piñon-juniper assemblage in and around the arroyo channel. The piedmont at its easternmost edge in the vicinity of the pueblo is characterized by a piñon-juniper lifezone, which grades into juniper-shortgrass plains at lower altitudes west of the mountains. The first two parallel rows of foothills of the Sangre de Cristo Mountains are covered with dense stands of piñon and juniper trees. The area between the second and third rows of hills as one moves eastward to higher elevations exhibits a

55

piñon-juniper–ponderosa pine ecotone lifezone. A true ponderosa lifezone exists only on the extreme margins of the Arroyo Hondo natural district along the crest of the third row of foothills.

Arable land in the district is concentrated in four areas: (1) the bottoms and sides of Arroyo Hondo Canyon and its various side canyons; (2) the Cañada Ancha wash, a narrow intermittent stream on the southern end of the natural district; (3) the piedmont; and (4) the runoff channels and shallow valleys between the Sangre de Cristo foothills.

The spring-fed floodplain areas of the main Arroyo Hondo Canyon seem to offer the greatest agricultural potential, with the canyon sides and the bottoms and sides of its tributary canyons running a close second. The danger of flooding here probably necessitated the planting of additional fields outside the canyon. The damage that such flooding can inflict was amply illustrated during the summer of 1971 when the runoff from an extremely heavy rainfall washed away a concrete and brick pumphouse built in the canyon below Arroyo Hondo Pueblo in 1926.

Farming in the broad, shallow-channeled Cañada Ancha wash would probably have been of the floodwater diversion variety described by Hack (1942:30), Forde (1931), and others that was practiced on the bottoms and low flood terraces of large arroyos. Crop washouts would, of course, have been a problem here also and would have been coupled with uncertainty about moisture due to the intermittent streamflow. A modern garden plot located on the floodplain of this wash during the summer of 1971 had to be irrigated regularly with well water.

Cultivation on the piedmont was practiced in the vicinity of Arroyo Hondo Pueblo up until some years before World War II. The cessation of this cultivation is attributed by various local people to a decline in rainfall over the last generation or so. Since modern farming equipment was presumably used on the piedmont, the fact of this former cultivation cannot be taken as prima facie evidence that the area was farmed during the prehistoric period. However, it does indicate that, given enough rainfall, the piedmont can be farmed. Finally, the runoff channels and shallow valleys between the foothills no doubt could have been used for small fields in the manner described by Hack for the Hopi (1942:26–29).

Twelve sites are known from this district. Occupation apparently began here no earlier than the Late Phase of the Developmental Period. However, during a short period from sometime before A.D. 1300 until about A.D. 1400, the district supported one of the largest sites in the area, Arroyo Hondo Pueblo.

4. Tetilla Canyon

This natural district is located in and around Tetilla Canyon, which carries runoff from the area on the western edge of La Bajada Mesa immediately north of Tetilla Peak and south of Cerro Colorado. Tetilla Arroyo, which drains the canyon, is a tributary of La Cañada de Cochiti Arroyo, which runs north of the Santa Fe River and ultimately joins the Rio Grande.

The physiography within this province includes two zones: (1) the mesa tops above the canyon, and (2) the narrow canyon bottom and sides.

Three lifezones occur in this district. The mesa tops on La Bajada Mesa proper support a shortgrass plains community; the canyon edges and sides a piñon-juniper assemblage. The bottom of Tetilla Canyon is dotted with springs around which various elements of the riparian lifezone are concentrated. At the far western end of the canyon near its mouth these springs disappear, and the canyon bottom supports a shortgrass plains lifezone with scattered juniper trees.

Arable land in this natural province is found in three areas: (1) the canyon bottom in the vicinity of the various springs found there, (2) the Tetilla Arroyo floodplain, terraces, and tributary arroyo canyons, and (3) the mesa flats above the canyon.

Soils in the arroyo would readily be resupplied with nutrients from periodic flooding and would thus be sufficiently rich to support crops. Fields in the vicinity of the springs would have the additional advantage of a high water table and would probably not have to be irrigated. As has been noted previously, however, the canyon bottom would be subject to periodic flooding and potential crop loss.

Crops planted on the mesas above the canyon in the vicinity of site LA 5 probably depended on both rainfall and the diversion of runoff in the channel of the arroyo, which cuts across the mesa and empties into Tetilla Canyon. None of the three potential agricultural areas in the natural district is large, a limiting factor on

57

the size of the population that could be supported there. Further, unlike the agricultural lands in the Rio Grande and Santa Fe River Canyon natural districts, the land in the Tetilla Canyon district is dependent on precipitation in the immediate vicinity, both directly, as rainfall and runoff, and indirectly in the recharge of the canyon springs.

Eleven sites are known from this natural district, only one of which dates to the Late Phase of the Developmental or the Early Phase of the Coalition Period. Occupation was not continuous after that time but either terminated or became sporadic until the Early Phase of the Classic Period. During the Middle Phase of the Classic Period the district apparently became heavily populated, with the settlement of LA 5 and several other sites. At the end of that phase, however, it once again became virtually empty until its Historic Period reoccupation.

5. The Middle Arroyo Hondo Drainage

This district is located on the western end of the postulated Arroyo Hondo Pueblo sustaining area along the middle course of the Arroyo Hondo between the Atchison, Topeka and Santa Fe railroad tracks on the east and the Albuquerque–Santa Fe highway (U.S. 85) on the west. The district consists of a roughly circular area no more than 1.5 miles in diameter.

The physiography of this province includes two zones: (1) the Arroyo Hondo floodplain, and (2) the low bluffs and sides of the arroyo canyon (Fig. 6).

The two lifezones in this area are a shortgrass plains assemblage in the arroyo floodplain and on the flats above it, and clusters of juniper trees mixed with shortgrass plains species in the side arroyos that dissect the low bluffs along the canyon edge. There is evidence that the present grassland domination of the natural district is fairly recent. Work in the area by the U.S. Geological Survey revealed the existence of a "perched water table" (Spiegel and Baldwin 1963:Plate 7) in the arroyo channel at this point that in earlier times might have allowed the establishment of a more mesic plant community. A perched water table is one that because of special, subsurface geological conditions is closer to the surface of the ground than would be expected in a particular area.

FIG. 6.   Natural District 5: The Middle Arroyo Hondo Drainage

Potentially arable land within this natural district is found in three areas: (1) the Arroyo Hondo floodplain in the vicinity of the perched water table, (2) the side arroyos dissecting the low bluffs, and (3) the flats above the arroyo on the bluff tops.

Presumably, the perched water table made farming possible on the floodplain along this portion of the Arroyo Hondo's course. Although crop loss through flooding would have been a danger here, it probably would have been far less important a risk than in the upper Arroyo Hondo canyon. Under present conditions, this far downstream the arroyo floods on a large and damaging scale only about once every generation. According to the present owner, a small vegetable garden was planted on the floodplain during the 1920s but was irrigated with water from a well, sunk to a depth of about 90 feet, on the floodplain.

Presumably the mouths of the small side arroyos that dissect the bluffs along the sides of the arroyo canyon could have been cultivated in the present manner of certain southwestern Indian groups (cf. Forde 1931; Hack 1942). These arroyos are very short, however,

59

and such use might have been difficult. The flat land above the arroyo on the bluffs might also have been cultivated, but such fields would have had to depend on rainfall or pot irrigation, since no large runoff channels for diversion cross the flats.

Three sites are reported from this natural district. The two that can be dated fall in the Late Phase of the Developmental Period and seem to cluster on the edge of the perched water table. Thus, it would appear that this natural district was habitable for only a rather restricted period, perhaps as a result of fluctuations in the special hydrological conditions at this spot.

6. The Canyon at the Edge of La Bajada Mesa

This natural district is located on the western edge of La Bajada Mesa between Tetilla Canyon on the north and the Santa Fe River Canyon on the south. Physiographically it consists of two zones: (1) the sides of La Bajada Mesa in the vicinity of the canyon and the sides of the canyon itself, and (2) the flat plain on the top of La Bajada Mesa in the vicinity of the canyon (Fig. 7).

FIG. 7. Natural District 6: The Canyon at the Edge of La Bajada Mesa. Santa Fe River in foreground.

The lifezones of these two zones are similar. The mesa top supports a shortgrass plains assemblage; the sides of the mesa and the canyon support about the same community, with the addition of scattered juniper trees that have gained a foothold among the large basaltic rocks.

Agricultural potential here seems very limited or even nonexistent. Although the soil is probably sufficiently rich in nutrients to support crops, rainfall is scant and there is no perennially available surface water. Floodwater farming *might* have been practiced on the top in the one arroyo with a fairly broad channel that drains into the canyon. Such farming would have required greater precipitation than prevails today.

There are eight sites in this district, clearly marginal to the major settlements clustered in the other natural districts. They include petroglyph sites, an apparent shrine, some unidentified structures, and a single rock-shelter. Prehistoric settlement does not seem to have begun here before the Early Phase of the Classic Period and apparently terminated by the Middle Phase of that period. Historic Period reoccupation was probably connected with cattle herding. An abandoned concrete stock tank and a modern earth dam, built here in connection with the cattle industry, indicate that the water runoff in the vicinity is significant.

7. *The Remaining Area of the Transect*

This natural district consists of the land intervening between the other six natural districts in the transect between the sustaining area on the east and the Rio Grande on the west. In includes three physiographic zones: (1) the rolling, westward-sloping piedmont, which begins at the edge of the Sangre de Cristo foothills and descends to the east side of the junction of Arroyo Hondo and Cienega Creek; (2) the plains at the top of La Bajada Mesa, except those portions included in other natural districts; and (3) the rugged hills atop La Bajada Mesa.

One major lifezone, the shortgrass plains, and one ecotone community, the shortgrass plains–piñon-juniper border, characterize this natural district. The piedmont physiographic subdivision supports the ecotone community. The piñon-juniper lifezone gradually thins as it descends from the Sangre de Cristo foothills to the plains until about

61

midway between the foothills and the Santa Fe River the zone gives way to true shortgrass plains with some scattered junipers. The top of La Bajada Mesa is almost totally dominated by the shortgrass plains assemblage, although juniper trees in varying densities occur on the slopes and near arroyos on the rugged hills.

The agricultural potential of this zone is extremely low and seems poorer the farther away one moves from the edge of the Sangre de Cristo foothills. It is not inconceivable that some of the arroyo channels that crosscut the piedmont might have been farmed under better rainfall conditions, but no evidence of such exploitation or settlement was found here during the 1971 survey. In general, the surface areas in this natural district lack dependable sources of water, at least under present conditions.

The scattered evidence of human use of this zone consists of a few small lithic scatters and occasional petroglyphs. Occupation seems to have picked up somewhat during the last 100 years, in conjunction with the cattle industry.

THE MODEL OF SETTLEMENT CHANGE

Once the natural districts were defined and ranked in terms of their human carrying capacity as inferred from their respective site weight totals, we attempted to reconstruct their settlement history. The potential of a natural district varies in terms of two factors: its physical attributes, especially the source of its water supply, and the level of technology of its inhabitants. By plotting these two variables on a graph we can represent the "trajectory" of the changing levels of human carrying capacity in the district through time. This attempt formed the basis of the alternative model of settlement change in the study area, which replaced the descredited Khuzistan model (Dickson 1975).

The earliest agricultural settlements in the study area occurred during the Early Phase of the Developmental Period, and were all concentrated in the two natural districts that we had classified as possessing primary exploitative potential, the Rio Grande floodplain and terraces and the Santa Fe River Canyon. By the Middle Phase of the Developmental Period, population had begun to spread into an area of secondary potential, the Upper Arroyo Hondo Canyon natural district. The Late Phase of the Developmental Period saw the colonization of the other secondary natural district in the survey area, Tetilla Canyon. Settlement of the tertiary Middle Arroyo Hondo drainage natural district also occurred at some point in the Late Phase of this period. The marginal area (the intermittently watered canyon on the western edge of La Bajada Mesa) was not definitely exploited before the Early Phase of the Classic Period, but petroglyphs and other undatable surface manifestations suggest that the area may have received sporadic use before that time. The portion of the study area classified as submarginal for agricultural exploitation consisted chiefly of the land between the mountains and the major drainages, which supported a shortgrass plains lifezone. While the absence of sufficient water made this area unsuitable for permanent agricultural settlement at any time in our sequence, the area no doubt served as important hunting territory throughout the prehistoric period.

Presumably, this expansion of settlement in the study area reflects population growth and the corresponding need to bring more land under cultivation. The spread of agricultural peoples did not go unchecked in the Southwest until the arrival of the Spaniards. Beginning as early as A.D. 1000 in some portions of New Mexico, for example in the Navajo Reservoir District (Dittert, Hester, and Eddy 1961: 220), subtle changes in rainfall and climate patterns appear to have taken place that evidently were damaging to the precariously balanced Pueblo agricultural systems. By the mid-thirteenth century, the expansion of Pueblo agriculturalists had esssentially stopped, and population contraction had begun.

The data from the study area indicate that as population declined in the face of these presumed climatic oscillations, settlement contracted in the natural districts in the reverse order of expansion, with some variations. The earliest abandonment in the study area occured in the Late Phase of the Developmental Period in the Middle Arroyo Hondo drainage, a natural district classified as of tertiary exploitative potential. Abandonment occurred next in the Tetilla Canyon natural district during the Middle Phase of the Coalition Period. This natural district was classified as being of secondary exploitative potential, so its abandonment at this time is contrary to the predictions of our model. This exception is mitigated somewhat by the fact that the district was reoccupied at a slightly later date. The Tetilla Canyon natural district is further discussed subsequently.

63

By the end of the Early Phase of the Classic Period, the other major secondary natural district, the Upper Arroyo Hondo, was also virtually emptied of population. Occupation in the two primary natural districts in the study area was never completely terminated, but it steadily decreased from the Early Phase of the Classic into the Historic Period, with the exception of a small increase during the Middle Phase of the Classic Period. Within the study area, only the modern Indian pueblo of Cochiti survives as a reminder of the former substantial indigenous population.

Thus, with few exceptions, the data from our study area indicate that Pueblo agriculturalists colonized the primary natural districts first, the secondary ones next, the tertiary ones after that, and the marginal ones last. They abandoned the districts in the reverse order: tertiary ones first, secondary ones next, and finally primary ones to some degree. This sequence of events is not unexpected. Birdsell (1967), Zubrow (1971:130), and others predict that population growth, upon approaching local carrying capacity, will tend to generate pressure toward outmigration. That settlement abandonment should follow the reverse order seems consistent with their work.

Two natural districts within the study area depart from this pattern. Tetilla Canyon, abandoned during the Early Phase of the Coalition Period, was reoccupied for 70 or more years during the Middle Phase of the Classic Period, at which time it supported a large population at a single pueblo site, Las Aguajes (LA 5). While this reoccupation cannot be explained satisfactorily under the terms of this model, perhaps an understanding of the brief return to Tetilla Canyon can be found in Clarke's notion that an adaptive system faced with environmental changes that upset its equilibrium will begin "scanning" or searching among alternatives for a solution, or strategy, to bring it back into its former equilibrium state. Such scanning may mean that the system will find itself in a number of nonequilibrium states before the appropriate course can be found (Clarke 1968:52–53, 93).

Perhaps the people who settled Las Aguajes immigrated to Tetilla Canyon in the face of environmental stress seeking a restoration of their former "equilibrium state" with their environment (or, as Arthur Jelinek remarked to me, perhaps they just wanted to keep eating). In either case, while they apparently found a temporary solution to their agricultural difficulties, after a time the resources of this secondary natural district probably proved insufficient to their needs.

The second exception to the pattern of our model is the time of occupation of the marginal natural district in the unnamed canyon at the western edge of La Bajada Mesa. The occupation and abandonment of this area fall sometime between the Early and Middle phases of the Classic Period, later than we would predict for a marginal district. While the late occupation of this district could conceivably be "scanning" as in the case of Tetilla Canyon, it is perhaps more likely that the area was never exploited agriculturally but remained a kind of peripheral manifestation of some other as yet poorly understood activity.

Once the general pattern of occupation had been recognized, an attempt was made to formalize it into a set of hypothetical statements about the population history of the study area. Such a set of hypotheses was sought both to replace the original model, which had been found untenable, and to provide a more general model for settlement pattern change that could be tested outside the study area. This second set of hypotheses is as follows.

Hypothesis 1

There is a correlation in any given natural district in the middle northern Rio Grande region between the presence of sites dating to the earliest phase of agricultural settlement in the region and a cultural sequence extending unbroken from the time of initial settlement until after A.D. 1542. Conversely, there is a correlation in any given natural district between the absence of sites dating to the earliest phase of agricultural settlement in the region and a cultural sequence that terminates prior to A.D. 1542.

Hypothesis 2

There is a correlation in any given natural district in the middle northern Rio Grande region between the location of the major habitation sites and the location of present supplies of perennially available water.

Hypothesis 3

There is a correlation in any given natural district in the middle northern Rio Grande region between the nature of the available water supply and the order of settlement by agricultural peoples in the various natural districts during times of population expansion. Specifically, agricultural settlement occurs earliest in those natural districts watered by perennial streamflow, next in those watered by perennial springs, and last in those with only intermittently available water.

Hypothesis 4

There is a correlation in the middle northern Rio Grande region between the nature of the available water supply and the order of abandonment of the various natural districts during times of population contraction. Specifically, settlement is abandoned earliest in those natural districts with only intermittently available water, next in those watered by perennial springs, and last, if at all, in those watered by perennial streamflow.

Hypothesis 5

Through the period of single increase and decrease in population in the northern middle Rio Grande region between A.D. 600 and A.D. 1542, areas of tertiary and marginal water resources were occupied in direct proportion to the total size of the population at any time.

5

Conclusions

AN INTERPRETATION OF ARROYO
HONDO PUEBLO PREHISTORY

This study began as an attempt to test one model of settlement distribution change and ended with the rejection of that model and the generation of an alternative one. Although the second model seems to hold for our survey area, no pretense is made that it has been demonstrated or verified. Testing in adjacent areas is necessary before we can elevate it to a second-level theory with relevance for the northern Rio Grande at large. However, both the model and the natural district concept upon which it is based are useful in interpreting the patterns of settlement and population change at Arroyo Hondo Pueblo.

Arroyo Hondo Pueblo is located in the Upper Arroyo Hondo natural district, a subarea that has been defined as of secondary exploitative potential or, rather, of a second order of human carrying capacity. Although this natural district lacks the broad, arable floodplains and large volumes of perennially available flowing water common to the primary natural districts of the Santa Fe River Canyon and Rio Grande floodplain and terraces, its perennial springs and rich, if somewhat limited, canyon bottom soil make it superior to the tertiary and marginal natural districts in the region.

Prior to about A.D. 1250, the Upper Arroyo Hondo natural district supported a small population at a few scattered sites. Sometime around A.D. 1300 the population in the district grew to very large proportions, first at two sites and finally at one large pueblo site. Traditionally, the rapid growth in size at certain Middle and Late

Phase Coalition Period sites has been explained as the result of im-migration from outside the region (Wendorf and Reed 1955:161; McNutt 1969). While this explanation is plausible, our alternative model would lead us to expect that areas of secondary exploitative potential like the Upper Arroyo Hondo natural district would have received the populations being forced by environmental stress to abandon tertiary and marginal natural districts within the northern Rio Grande region itself. However, it remains to be demonstrated that the possible relocated local population was large enough to ac-count for the growth at Coalition Period sites that has been ob-served in the region. At present only two small sites (LA 191 and LA 10614) from the Late Phase of the Developmental Period are known to have been occupied in tertiary and marginal districts of our study area prior to the remarkable Middle and Late Coalition Period popu-lation increases. Unless more Early Coalition Period sites are found in tertiary and marginal districts outside the study area, we must conclude that immigration of local populations into the primary and secondary natural districts of the northern Rio Grande region would not have been sufficient to account for the population growth there. Thus, if this prediction of the model proves inadequate, we might have to invoke the mechanism of immigration of external peoples into the northern Rio Grande region after all.

In any event, early in the fifteenth century, this secondary natural district was abandoned as well. To interpret this phenom-enon in terms of the alternative model, it is necessary to expand our definitions of the Upper Arroyo Hondo natural district to in-clude the territory outside the study area north as far as modern Santa Fe and south as far as the Lamy cutoff of New Mexico Highway 84–85–285 (Interstate 25) along the foothills of the San-gre de Cristo Mountains. The distribution of sites within this ex-panded natural district forms an interesting pattern. Major sites dating to the first half of the fourteenth century, such as Pindi Pueblo (LA 1), Los Alamos Pueblo, and presumed settlements under modern Santa Fe, seem to have been spaced at roughly five-mile intervals in the vicinity of perennially available water at the point where the foothills and the piedmont join. It seems un-likely that this spacing is accidental. Rather, it would appear that these large, contemporaneous fourteenth-century sites had struck a balance between population and resources and, given the technical level at which they were operating, had reached the human carrying capacity of the natural district.

Let us for the moment consider these fourteenth-century pueblos not as individual sites but as components in a system exploiting the resources of the natural province in which they were located. Let us further assume that this exploitative system had reached a kind of optimal equilibrium point at which its food production was just equal to the requirements of its populations but any additional production would cause environmental degradation. Under such circumstances, we would expect this system, and its individual pueblo components, to be extremely vulnerable to any external changes that would affect the ability to produce food. Simply said, a society in which production equals the subsistence requirements of its population is in dire straits when production abruptly declines. If our initial assumption was correct, we may conclude that Arroyo Hondo Pueblo's precipitous decline and abandonment, together with the somewhat earlier decline in the surrounding sites in the province, were the result of just such a change in productivity, induced perhaps by climatic change.

Although it is impossible to trace the former inhabitants of Arroyo Hondo Pueblo after the abandonment of the site, it seems likely that they remained in the general area. In fact, we observe a slight increase in the site weight totals in the transect (see Table 3) during the Middle Phase of the Classic Period that partly postdates the abandonment of Arroyo Hondo Pueblo. In terms of our model, we would predict that the people leaving secondary natural districts would fall back on the primary ones. However, an examination of the site weight totals for the Middle Phase of the Classic Period on a district-by-district basis (see Table 4) does not support such a prediction. The primary natural districts in the study area, the Rio Grande floodplain and terraces and the Santa Fe River Canyon, show continued decline at this time. Instead, growth is seen in a secondary natural district, Tetilla Canyon, which had apparently been largely abandoned at a much earlier date.

In the discussion of the alternative model, this slightly anomalous growth was referred to as possible "scanning behavior" on the part of the cultural system. It is also possible that the Rio Grande natural district was closed to refugees by the occupants, who were feeling the effects of the apparent agricultural difficulties as well. In any case, the net increase in the Tetilla Canyon natural district during the Middle Phase of the Classic Period is slightly less than one-third of the corrected site weight total for the Upper Arroyo Hondo natural district during the last phase of occupation at the main site there. The increase in this natural district is suggestive and perhaps offers a clue to the ultimate fate of the Arroyo Hondo people.

Aside from this oscillation in site weight totals during the middle of the Classic Period (Table 3), the population curve in the Upper Arroyo Hondo natural district exhibits a trend of growth and decline generally similar to that of the transect (which is based on site weight data that do not include the Upper Arroyo Hondo natural district). Population growth in both the Upper Arroyo Hondo district and the transect peaks during the Late Phase of the Coalition Period, but the dramatic increase begins earlier in the transect (during the Early Phase of the Coalition), suffers a slight decline at the time shortly before Arroyo Hondo Pueblo begins its ascendance (the Middle Phase of the same period), and then drops off in a more abrupt fashion throughout the later Classic Period.

AN INTERPRETATION OF NORTHERN RIO GRANDE PREHISTORY

The following section attempts to apply our natural district model of settlement pattern to the northern Rio Grande region as a whole. At the risk of seeming either redundant or overcautious, however, it is necessary to reiterate that the model remains untested beyond a very limited portion of the region and that no effort has been made to collate the mass of existing site data that would be necessary for the model's systematic application beyond our study area. Further, existing evidence from at least one area within the region, the Galisteo Basin, seems at odds with some of the model's specific predictions. Nonetheless, the application of the model to the northern Rio Grande at large does seem to produce certain insights into the process of cultural change there. If these insights serve as the basis for or stimulus to additional research in the region, this most tentative effort will be justified.

Existing research suggests that the transition to settled agriculture in the northern Rio Grande region began around A.D. 600 (Wendorf and Reed 1955). We would hypothesize that this early exploitation and settlement took place in the primary natural districts in the region. Population growth during the Early Phase of the Developmental Period between A.D. 600 and A.D. 900 was probably slow over much of the region as the new agricultural technology was adjusted to the northern Rio Grande environment. When this adjustment had been made, however, the population no doubt began to make substantial increases.

Within the study area, settlement had begun to spread into the secondary and, to some extent, the tertiary natural districts by the Middle Phase of the Developmental Period between A.D. 900 and A.D.1100. Further, the site weight totals in the study area appear nearly to have doubled every century. During the Late Phase of the same period, the growth rate was even more accelerated and the population grew to four times its size of the preceding phase, that is, the population appears to have doubled every half-century. If we may extrapolate from evidence of site weight and gross increases in site numbers in the study area, we must conclude that the population history in the northern Rio Grande region at this time was also characterized by dramatic, even geometric, expansion and growth.

The temptation is to account for this growth within the study area, and perhaps the region at large, as due to the influx of immigrants. However, despite the fact that the northern Rio Grande region seems at this time to have been part of a general Chaco–San Juan "interaction sphere," to use Glassow's phrase, with which it shares many stylistic traits, there is little particularly convincing evidence of immigrations into the Rio Grande from those regions (Wendorf and Reed 1955:144).

Rather, the population increases of the Developmental Period seem not unlike what ecologists expect to observe in the populations of species newly introduced into a favorable environment. According to Gerkins (1969:402), in such situations a period of exponential growth occurs, and the population of the new species spreads and grows until it reaches the carrying capacity of the new environment. Certainly such a model does not seem out of place in accounting for the rapid growth and spread of the agricultural peoples in the favorable northern Rio Grande environment during the Developmental Period.

71

Further, a large part of this population growth may be attributable to the refinement and introduction of improved strains of maize in the Southwest after about A.D. 700 (Carter 1945). Schoenwetter and Dittert characterize these new strains as "larger, higher yielding per plant and more drought resistant. Such maize made smaller plots more productive and could be grown under a greater number of conditions" (1968:49).

If this reconstruction of the population growth and expansion in the Developmental Period in the northern Rio Grande region is valid, we might make four assumptions about the agricultural technology of the times:

1. Its increased productivity was sufficient to generate population growth.

2. It was "extensive" in that it demanded a relatively large amount of land per capita to support that population.

3. Given the "extensive" nature of the agricultural technology, population growth generated enough stress on critical resources (such as arable land and water) to necessitate exploitation of land beyond the primary natural districts.

4. The new strains of maize were, as Schoenwetter and Dittert note, capable of being grown under a greater number of conditions than the earlier strains, making expansion into the less favored natural provinces both possible and fairly attractive (1968).

With the onset of the Coalition Period around A.D. 1200, we note two new trends in population and settlement pattern in our study area (Table 1). First, a large increase occurred in the site weight totals for the Early Phase of the Coalition Period between A.D. 1200 and A.D. 1250. Although corrected site weight totals for the study area dip slightly during the succeeding Middle Phase, during the Late Phase of the Coalition Period these totals jump to a figure more than 17 times the total at the end of the Developmental Period. Correlated with this growth is a new trend in settlement patterning involving abandonment of the tertiary and some secondary

72

natural districts. That is, the tremendous growth in the site weight totals occurred together with a decrease in the number of sites outside the primary natural provinces and a slight increase in the gross numbers within it. Of course, Smiley, Stubbs, and Bannister (1953) and Fritts (1965:429) cite evidence of a marked curtailment in tree-ring growth in the northern Rio Grande region between about A.D. 1245 and A.D. 1295, which apparently indicates that drought conditions prevailed there from around the end of the Early Phase until just before the end of the Middle Phase of the Coalition Period. It thus appears likely that during much of the thirteenth century the northern Rio Grande witnessed:

1. Stress of some kind (presumably environmental), which rendered ineffective the extensive agriculture presumed to have been practiced during the Developmental Period.

2. A return to and greater aggregation within the primary and certain secondary natural districts, correlated with the abandonment of the tertiary and marginal provinces.

That is, we conclude that environmental stress on agricultural production temporarily reduced the human carrying capacity of the middle northern Rio Grande and thus was the prime cause of the abandonment of those natural districts within it that were of less than primary or secondary exploitative potential. Populations abandoning these presumably inferior zones are assumed to have emigrated to the natural provinces of superior exploitative potential within the same region.

The tertiary and marginal natural districts are characterized by intermittent or somewhat unpredictable water supplies; the primary and secondary zones by perennial sources of water. We hypothesize that the extensive agriculture of the Developmental Period made use of a wide variety of arable land and water sources in much the same fashion as the modern Hopi (Hack 1942:26–38; Bradfield 1971). Such practices would facilitate the expansion of settlement into the tertiary and marginal natural districts and, at a given level of climatic stability, might give them an agricultural yield and human carrying capacity comparable in many ways to the secondary natural districts.

A marked change in climatic conditions—such as a shift in the annual rainfall pattern—would affect the productivity of extensive agriculture in *all* the natural districts. However, it would presumably be far more harmful to that of the tertiary zones directly dependent for water on intermittent rainfall in their immediate vicinity than to that of the primary and secondary zones perennially watered by the runoff of springs and streams draining a far larger area. Thus, climatic stress would affect the carrying capacity earliest and hardest in the tertiary and marginal districts, latest and least in the secondary and then the primary ones.

Productivity would decline, albeit to a lesser degree, in those favored districts as well. This decline, coupled with the additional strain on resources generated by the presumed influx of farmers abandoning the less favorable natural districts, might have created in the primary and secondary natural provinces the kinds of population pressure on critical resources described by Boserup (1965) as a prerequisite for the development of *intensive* agricultural practices in place of extensive ones. In fact, we do observe in the transect of our study area a slight population decline during the Middle Phase of the Coalition Period (Table 3), which may have been caused by such stress or pressure on resources.

If population pressure of this kind did force the thirteenth-century farmers of the northern Rio Grande to seek to increase productivity by intensifying their cultivation through use of irrigation and other measures, they would not have had to look far to borrow techniques with which to do so. The peoples of Mesa Verde (Rohn 1963; Stewart and Donnelly 1943), Chaco Canyon (Vivian 1970), southeastern Arizona (Gladwin et al. 1937; Haury 1936), and northern Mexico (Johnson 1960) all seem to have practiced hydraulic management at an earlier date than the post-A.D. 1200 Coalition Period development proposed here. Participation in the same "interaction sphere" with Chaco Canyon and the San Juan region could have provided the inhabitants of the Rio Grande with knowledge of such practices long before they put them into practice. They were apparently not adopted earlier here because, as the Developmental Period colonization of the tertiary and marginal zones seems to indicate, until the thirteenth century extensive agriculture was so sufficiently productive without the addition of elaborate irrigation systems that there was little adaptive advantage to spur their implementation.

If these techniques of intensive agriculture were in fact borrowed from the Mesa Verde region, the ceramics and architectural styles from there that became popular in the northern Rio Grande region during the Coalition Period may have been linked with these techniques in some ideological manner and adopted as part of a single complex. In other words, the actual presence of Mesa Verdeans in the northern Rio Grande at this time might not be needed to explain the presence of elements of their material culture here.

We have presented no hard evidence that the transformation from extensive to intensive irrigation agriculture first took place in the northern Rio Grande during the Coalition Period. Instead we have suggested that the probable inability of the extensive agricultural techniques to cope with the drought conditions of the last half of the thirteenth century, coupled with the pressure on critical resources created by population immigration and aggregation within the secondary and primary natural districts, seems likely to have created the necessary preconditions for such an event. Further, intensive techniques would not have had to be developed in vacuo in the northern Rio Grande, since systems that could have been drawn upon as models existed among contemporaneous groups in surrounding regions.

In summary, the Coalition Period in the northern Rio Grande region appears to have been characterized by the following events:

1. Environmental stress that forced the abandonment of the tertiary and marginal natural districts by reducing the human carrying capacity of the region and rendering extensive agriculture possible only in the primary and secondary natural districts.

2. The aggregation of populations within the primary and secondary natural districts of the region.

3. Population pressure on critical resources within the primary and secondary natural districts caused by the combined effects of continued environmental stress and population aggregation. This pressure in turn yielded:

   a. A slight initial population decline in the Middle Phase of the Coalition Period in the crowded primary and secondary natural districts.

b. The transformation of the extensive agricultural systems into intensive ones in those natural districts at least by the Late Phase of the Coalition Period.

c. The reestablishment of an equilibrium between population and productivity in those natural districts where intensive agriculture could be practiced.

4. The near quadrupling of population during the Late Phase of the Coalition Period due to the return of more favorable climatic conditions between A.D. 1300 and A.D. 1320 (Smiley, Stubbs, and Bannister 1953; Fritts 1965) and the success of the new, intensive agricultural adaptation presumably developed or adopted during the preceding phase.

However, in our study area at least, this population growth trend did not continue unabated throughout the subsequent Early Phase of the Classic Period. If we may generalize to the middle northern Rio Grande region at large, a marked population decline had taken place there by the end of the Early Phase. Decline at this time is more difficult to correlate with the dendroclimatic curve. Data collected by Smiley, Stubbs, and Bannister (1953:54–55) and Fritts (1965:430) suggest that, while tree-ring growth between A.D. 1320 and A.D. 1350 was not good, it was not extremely bad either. Yet the effects of environmental stress on a society can be calculated only by including population size and subsistence needs in the equation. A social group whose population has expanded to a point approaching the carrying capacity of its environment might be devastated by environmental stress of a magnitude that it could have weathered earlier in its history when its population was smaller and its productivity not at maximum. The fact that Arroyo Hondo Pueblo appears to have suffered population decline or even partial or full abandonment at approximately A.D. 1350 suggests that the economy of the pueblo was at a point where even a moderate decline in growing conditions was sufficient to trigger disaster. Despite the fact that the tree-ring data suggest that the years after A.D. 1350 were quite favorable ones for tree growth, Arroyo Hondo Pueblo apparently did not experience population renewal until after A.D. 1370. The final abandonment of that site before A.D. 1425 (Schwartz and Lang 1973:30–32) is correlated with the beginning of a period of severe inhibition in tree-ring growth observed by Fritts (1965:430) for the years after A.D. 1410 until about the end of the fifteenth century. It seems likely that what happened to Arroyo Hondo Pueblo occurred more generally in the northern Rio Grande region, that is, that the success of the new, intensive adaptation allowed population to grow to such proportions that when a minor climatic oscillation slightly reduced the human carrying capacity of the region, the adaptive systems collapsed entirely.

Although this collapse presumably began at the early end of the Middle Phase of the Classic Period, its full effects are not measurable in our study area site weight totals until the following Late Phase when our figures drop to one-sixth their Middle Phase level (see Table 1). Population history during the Late Phase of the Classic Period in the northern Rio Grande region seems to have been characterized by three major events. First, there was a general and progressive population decline, which continued until the Spanish Entrada. This decline is correlated with oscillations in tree-ring growth observed in the upper Rio Grande region (Fritts 1965:430) as well as with the evidence of a worldwide climatic deterioration in the sixteenth century (Bryson and Julian 1962). Second, there appears to have been a general abandonment of the secondary natural districts in favor of more or less exclusive settlement in the primary ones. Finally, near the end of the Classic Period, it is likely that the spread of European diseases in advance of actual contact may have contributed to this decline.

Notes

1. The term "lifezone" is synonymous with the "biotic community" defined by Gerkins as "a natural assemblage of organisms in a given habitat" (1969:402). As Gerkins notes, this definition lacks precision due to the shallowness of our understanding of intraspecies relationships within such lifezones. Nevertheless,

> definite mental images are formed when tropical rain forest, tundra, desert, grassland, deciduous forest and evergreen forest are mentioned. Each term calls to mind a particular kind of natural assemblage of plants, different from the other. A community is a definite entity, with its own characteristic structure and species composition (Gerkins 1969:402).

Presumably, the nature and distribution of lifezones are determined by certain properties of the physical world acting in combination. These properties or factors include solar radiation (Shelford 1963:10), climatic factors such as mean annual temperatures, precipitation, and evapotranspiration rate (Holdridge 1964:17–30), and edaphic factors including soil type, available nutrients, and occurrence of fire (Boughley 1968:17–22). As Boughley (1968:3–4) notes:

> It may be postulated that the establishment of a particular organism in a given area is dependent upon the availability of the necessary elements in the required minimum quantity and the functioning of critical physical factors at the required minimum level, combined with the occurrence of these elements and the operation of these factors within the tolerance limits of the organism. (1968:3–4)

Since the "necessary elements" are not infinite in number and their occurrence is not random across the face of the earth but is generally continuous and predictable, the recurrent biotic associations, or "lifezones," that result from the various finite combinations of these elements are usually also continuous and predictable. Given specific data on the successive states of the necessary elements in an area, the ecological zonation in that area may be generally predicted. Conversely, it is possible to use the actual ecological zonation to work backward to knowledge of the necessary elements in the environment that determine them. The accurate plotting of this zonation occupied much of the time of N. Edmund Kelley, the ecologist working on the Arroyo Hondo project, and resulted in a detailed map of the ecological lifezones in the Santa Fe area (Kelley 1980:58).

2. A similar although more elegant solution to the problem of comparing sites in the Southwest has been independently developed by Plog (1975:97–98).

78

Appendix A

DELINEATION OF THE ARROYO HONDO SUSTAINING AREA

"Sustaining area" is defined here as the territory around any human settlement from which the primary sustenance of the community is drawn. For Pueblo sites this territory generally must have been capable of supporting certain wild and domestic plants and animals known from archaeological evidence to have been used by the inhabitants.

The identification of a pueblo's sustaining area is facilitated by the fact that domesticated plants like corn, beans, and squash cannot be grown everywhere but are limited to areas where their specific requirements for water, soil composition, frost-free days, and the like, are met. Wild resources, such as piñon trees (for nuts), deer, and antelope, have different requirements and wider adaptive ranges than domesticated plants, and their distribution is a predictable response to environmental parameters; they are member species of the recurrent natural associations or lifezones.

However, a sustaining area is not simply coterminous with either the boundaries of natural lifezones or the locations of nearby agricultural lands. In most instances, the extent to which the inhabitants of a pueblo could actually exploit such areas was probably conditioned by realpolitik. Thus, size and location of adjacent sites must be considered vis-à-vis the site in question in any attempt to define its sustaining area.

To define the sustaining area for Arroyo Hondo Pueblo, we used existing archaeological and ethnological accounts (e.g., Whiting 1939; Hack 1942; Ford 1972) to gauge the importance of various wild and domestic plant species in the Pueblo economy. These estimates, together with existing data on the topography and hydrology of the Santa Fe area and the preliminary results of the survey of its present-day ecology, which was under way at the time of our study, allowed a very rough determination of (1)the location of the areas of primary, secondary, and marginal agricultural potential around the site and (2) the location of the natural lifezones in the vicinity. Preliminary results of the ecological survey conducted by Edmund Kelley revealed that Arroyo Hondo Pueblo was located in the narrowest portion of the piñon-juniper belt of the southern Sangre de Cristo range. This location allowed for easy access to and use of the two adjacent vegetational zones, the shortgrass plains and the ponderosa pine forest. The importance of such access probably cannot be exaggerated. Its significance has been recognized in Guatemala (Coe and Flannery 1966, 1967), in the southeastern United States (Larson 1972:388–89), and elsewhere.

Regarding agricultural land in the vicinity of the pueblo, Kelley noted that a mean annual temperature of between 49 and 55 degrees Fahrenheit and an annual rainfall of between 14 and 18 inches, with much of the moisture concentrated in the critical months of July and August, are necessary for dry farming corn. Until the last decade before World War II, the piedmont area surrounding Arroyo Hondo Canyon met these requirements, albeit with a tendency toward drought.

The presence of perennial springs and the perpetual renewal of soil nutrients through periodic flooding make Arroyo Hondo Canyon one of the best spots in the study area, outside of the major river valleys, for practicing floodwater or simple irrigation farming. This land was considered to be of primary agricultural potential. Above and south of the canyon is a broad, intermittent stream called Cañada Ancha that would also offer an excellent site for such farming, provided rainfall conditions were somewhat better than at present. This area was classed as being of secondary agricultural potential. Finally, the foothills of the Sangre de Cristo Mountains east of the Arroyo Hondo site are dissected by a number of small to medium-sized runoff channels and shallow valleys. These areas very likely were exploited by agricultural techniques similar to modern Hopi *akchin* farming (Hack 1942:26–28). We classed these channels and the *bajada* as being of tertiary potential.

Next, archaeological sites in the vicinity of Arroyo Hondo Pueblo were plotted, together with lifezone and agricultural data, on a USGS map as a means of reconstructing the former sustaining area of the pueblo. The site itself is located above the springs and floodplain of Arroyo Hondo Canyon; the nearest land of equal agricultural potential under present climatic conditions is some 5 miles south of the site in Cañon Ancha around the springs known locally as Pueblo Well.

Lands of a slightly lower quality are situated in the Cañada de los Alamos arroyo about 0.75 mile southeast of Pueblo Well. Two major sites occur at these spots: Chamisa Locita (LA 4) in Cañon Ancha, and Los Alamos Pueblo (LA 8) in Cañada de los Alamos. The limited tree-ring material collected at these sites suggests that the occupation of Los Alamos occurred sometime from around A.D. 1243 to A.D. 1284 and of Chamisa Locita sometime from around A.D. 1313 to A.D. 1333 (Smiley, Stubbs, and Bannister 1953:15,17; Robinson, Harrill, and Warren 1973:31,112). On the basis of these data it appears that this area was occupied somewhat earlier than, and contemporaneously with, our site. Abandonment in this area seems to have preceded the abandonment in the vicinity of Arroyo Hondo Pueblo.

The territory between Arroyo Hondo and Cañon Ancha consists of a low range of hills running roughly parallel north to south at altitudes between 7,200 and 7,700 feet. These hills support an abundant piñon-juniper lifezone. To the east is a basin that slopes upward toward the main body of the Sangre de Cristo range; this basin is drained partly by Cañon Ancha and the smaller Cañada Ancha. To the west these foothills abut the piedmont. Around and out from their base, the piedmont supports a piñon-juniper lifezone. As one moves gradually westward, however, the forest assemblage gives way to an ecotone between it and the shortgrass plains lifezone, and it is the latter biotic community that dominates the piedmont from the edge of the ecotone to the Rio Grande floodplain.

The presence of sites LA 4 and LA 8 indicates that the agricultural land in the vicinity of Pueblo Well, Cañon Ancha, and Cañada de los Alamos was exploited by groups other than the inhabitants of

81

Arroyo Hondo Pueblo during much of that pueblo's occupation. Precisely who controlled the territory between the Pueblo Well area and the Arroyo Hondo Canyon was more difficult to determine because no archaeological sites from this area were known or recorded in the Laboratory of Anthropology site files. It seems likely, therefore, that this territory was a kind of buffer zone between the two primary agricultural areas. With this in mind, we divided the intervening territory roughly in half on the assumption that Cañada Ancha, which ran from east to west through the middle of the territory, was a very probable southern boundary for the Arroyo Hondo sustaining area and the northern boundary of the sustaining area of LA 4 and LA 8 (Map 4). The wash itself appeared to be of secondary agricultural potential, and the forested piñon-juniper area in the foothills on either side seemed to be of approximately similar hunting and gathering potential.

The northern limit of the Arroyo Hondo Pueblo sustaining area remains largely indeterminate. It no doubt extended into the modern city limits of Santa Fe, but the long historic occupation and recent expansion of the town have removed most traces of any prehistoric surface remains. The water resources and arable land along Arroyo de los Chamisos and the Santa Fe River, which run parallel to one another north of Arroyo Hondo Pueblo, certainly attracted aboriginal settlement and exploitation. However, the sherds and other debris that commonly crop up in construction foundation trenches north of the Plaza and elsewhere within Santa Fe can only hint at the extent of this former occupation. This fragmentary evidence is summarized and discussed in Appendix D. In any case, limited knowledge of what lies beneath modern Santa Fe, coupled with the encroachment of the city's outskirts into the area immediately above Arroyo Hondo Canyon, led us to limit our survey to about one mile beyond the northern edge of the canyon's rim.

The nearest primary agricultural land to the east of the site is about one mile upstream, where even under present conditions a spring or seep in the floor of Arroyo Hondo Canyon ensures a year-round water supply. On a low rise just above this spring stands the medium-sized Upper Arroyo Hondo Pueblo (LA 76). This site, dated by tree-ring evidence to between A.D. 1287 and A.D. 1316, was evidently occupied during the first quarter of settlement at Arroyo Hondo Pueblo (Smiley, Stubbs, and Bannister 1953:19–20). The

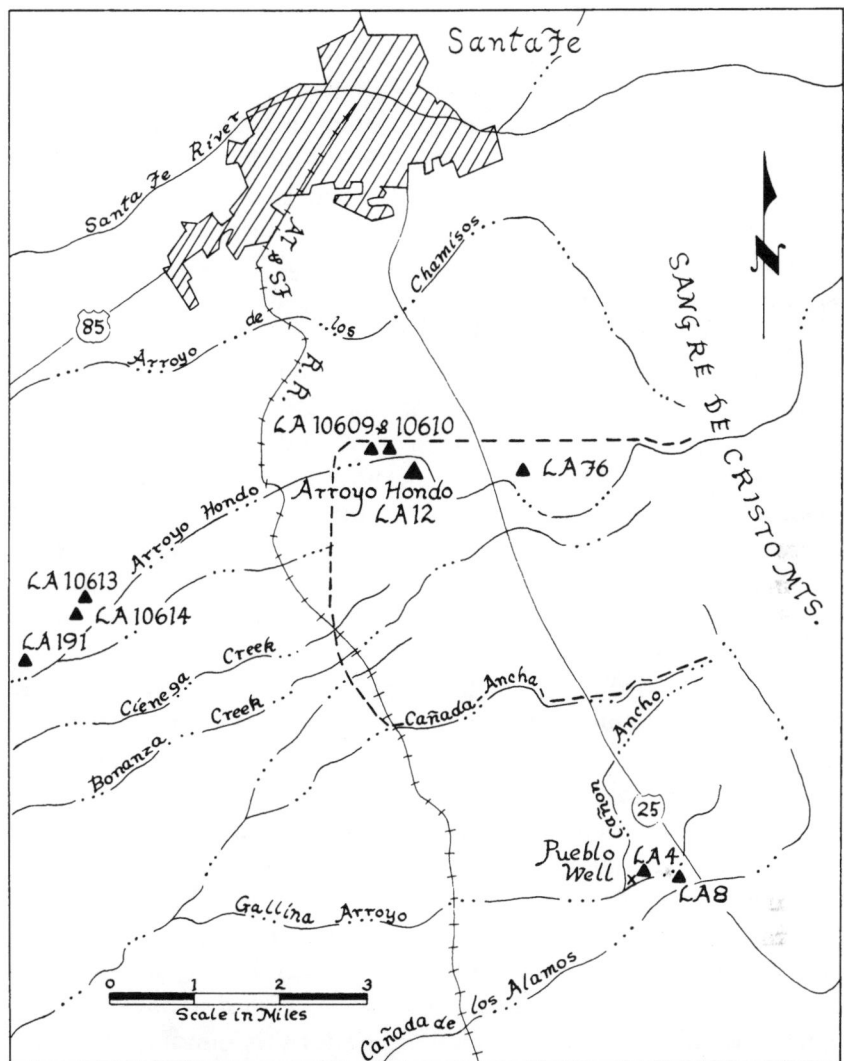

MAP 4. The Proposed Arroyo Hondo Sustaining Area. The dotted line marks the hypothesized boundary of the pueblo's agricultural territory.

proximity of the two sites seemed to complicate efforts at reconstructing the Arroyo Hondo Pueblo sustaining area. It was felt that unless the two sites were complementary parts of a single system, they would have been spaced farther apart. Additionally, one of the advantages of site placement in this area, where the piñon-juniper belt was so narrow, was access to the resources of the ponderosa pine zone. Thus, despite the presence of LA 76 on the east of Arroyo Hondo Pueblo, we concluded that the eastern boundary of the

83

sustaining area of the latter site was located somewhere *beyond* LA 76 in the ponderosa–piñon–juniper ecotone or in the ponderosa pine zone itself. No sites were on record in the Laboratory of Anthropology site files for either the ecotone or the ponderosa zone in the areas immediately east of Arroyo Hondo Pueblo. However, Wendorf and Miller discuss the presence of eight campsites at altitudes between 7,500 and 12,000 feet in other parts of the Sangre de Cristo Mountains. Four of these sites appeared to fall in the Early or Preceramic Period, but the remaining four contained a few, largely indistinguishable ceramics that placed them somewhere in the Pueblo stage from the Developmental to the Classic Period (1959:51).

These data may be taken as a good indication that the high mountain lifezones were exploited, probably by seasonal hunting groups, in search of plant resources, wood, building material, and animals such as wapiti. Thus, it was concluded that the eastern boundary of the sustaining area extended into the forest and tundra lifezones of the Sangre de Cristo Mountains, which were exploited for their wild resources.

When the Arroyo Hondo Pueblo sustaining area was first defined before the 1971 summer field season, the only known sites to the west within 5 miles were LA 191 ("Mocho") and LA 10609. The latter was a very small Historic Period site with a possible Early or Middle Phase Developmental Period component located downstream in the Arroyo Hondo canyon about 0.5 mile from the main site. The second site, LA 191, was about 3 miles west of the main pueblo on the banks of Arroyo Hondo and had produced a consistent series of tree-ring dates that placed its occupancy between A.D. 1115 and A.D. 1194 (Smiley, Stubbs, and Bannister 1953:25–26). Thus, these sites seemed to have been occupied and abandoned either before or after the founding of Arroyo Hondo Pueblo and, unlike LA 4 and LA 8, could be of little help in defining the sustaining area boundaries.

In light of this, we decided to survey the length of Arroyo Hondo as far west as LA 191 in an effort to discover sites contemporaneous with Arroyo Hondo Pueblo. The effort proved only partly successful, for although three sites were discovered, two of them, LA 10610 and LA 10613, lacked datable surface materials, and the third, LA 10614, had been occupied prior to Arroyo Hondo Pueblo.

It became apparent from this examination of Arroyo Hondo Canyon that the five sites within or along it were clustered in two locations.

Sites LA 10609 and LA 10610 were located within a mile of Arroyo Hondo Pueblo inside the narrow confines of the canyon itself; sites LA 191, LA 10613, and LA 10614 were situated on the banks of the arroyo about 5 miles west of the pueblo. The spacing of these clusters most likely bears a relationship to the arable land within the arroyo's course, assuming that the territory between the site clusters would be of a lower agricultural potential than that near the sites. If this is the case, the western limit of the agricultural lands within the Arroyo Hondo Pueblo sustaining area very likely lay somewhere between LA 10610 and LA 191, probably no more than a mile west of the main pueblo. If the small, presently undated, rectangular wall outline at LA 10609 should turn out to be the remains of a field building or "farmhouse" associated with the occupation of Arroyo Hondo Pueblo, the argument for placing the western boundary of the pueblo's agricultural lands in its vicinity would be strengthened.

It is possible that the lands in the vicinity of LA 191, LA 10613, and LA 10614 were farmed by peoples from Arroyo Hondo Pueblo after the abandonment of these three sites. This seems unlikely, since no ceramic evidence for post–Developmental Period use of the area has so far come to light. Beyond this cluster of sites, the nearest recorded settlements are located in and in front of the Santa Fe River Canyon more than 5 miles to the west.

Note that we have been careful to refer to the land just beyond site LA 10610 as the western boundary of the *agricultural* land in the sustaining area. This is because it seems almost certain that extensive use was made of the shortgrass plains lifezone both downstream beyond the agricultural land in the arroyo canyon and above the arroyo on the piedmont. Such a lifezone would offer hunters such ungulate species as antelope and possibly bison and wild plant species such as cactus, various tubers, saltbush and sagebrush for dyes and herbal remedies, and so forth. Thus, the western boundary of the pueblo's sustaining area probably was, like its eastern boundary in the mountains, an indeterminate extension onto the piedmont. Presumably such an area would have been used in common with the peoples of surrounding settlements.[1]

1. Using a similar method for a much larger area, Hammond (1972:772–78) attempts to reconstruct the "exploitation territory" surrounding the sites in the vicinity of Lubaantun in Belize by dividing the area between them into "Thiessen polygons."

Appendix B
BASIC SITE DATA (TABLES 5–7)

TABLE 5.
Sites in the Study Area

Site Number	Lifezone	Phases Present	Estimated Number of Structures	Site Weight	Natural District
LA 3	Shortgrass	Early Coalition	140 rooms	141.00	2
LA 5	Piñon-Juniper	Middle Classic	166 rooms	167.00	4
LA 7	Shortgrass	Early Coalition to Late Coalition	450–500 rooms, 4 kivas	76.55	2
LA 12	Piñon-Juniper	Late Coalition to Middle Classic	1,100 rooms, 5 or more kivas	501.66[a]	3
LA 16	Shortgrass	Early Coalition to Middle Classic; Historic	1,000 rooms, 2 kivas	126.00	2
LA 34	Shortgrass	Historic	18-room compound	19.00	1
LA 44	Shortgrass	Historic	Unknown	1.00	2
LA 55	Shortgrass	Early to Middle Developmental	Sherd scatter	1.00	1
LA 70	Unknown	Early Coalition to Late Classic	100 rooms, 8 kivas	35.66	1
LA 76	Piñon-Juniper	Early to Late Coalition	45–50 rooms	12.25	3
LA 113	Juniper-Short-grass	Early to Middle Developmental; Early Coalition	Unknown	1.00	1

[a]This site weight is based on an earlier estimate of 1,500 rooms, since the revised figure of 1,100 rooms was not available at the time this study was done.

87

TABLE 5. *Continued*

Site Number	Lifezone	Phases Present	Estimated Number of Structures	Site Weight	Natural District
LA 115	Riparian	Historic	Unknown	1.00	2
LA 126	Shortgrass	Late Developmental or Early Coalition to Historic	138 rooms	18.25	1
LA 148	Shortgrass	Late Developmental	2 rooms	3.00	2
LA 149	Riparian	Late Coalition to Early Classic	Unknown	1.00	2
LA 150	Shortgrass	Middle Developmental to Late Coalition	Unknown	1.00	2
LA 163	Shortgrass	Historic	Unknown	1.00	2
LA 164	Shortgrass	Middle Classic; Historic	4 rooms	3.00	2
LA 165	Riparian	Late Classic to Historic	Unknown	1.00	2
LA 166	Juniper-Shortgrass	Late Developmental	50–75 rooms, 7 kivas	58.00	2
LA 177	Riparian	Early Developmental	Sherd scatter	1.00	2
LA 191	Shortgrass	Late Developmental	4–6 pithouses	5.00	5
LA 230	Riparian	Early to Middle Developmental; Historic	Sherd scatter	1.00	2
LA 247	Shortgrass	Middle Developmental to Middle Coalition	75–100 rooms, 3 or more kivas	16.60	1
LA 249	Shortgrass	Early Developmental to Late Classic	150–200 rooms, 2–4 kivas	17.88	1
LA 256	Shortgrass, Riparian	Middle to Late Developmental	Sherd scatter	1.00	2

Site	Vegetation	Time period	Description		Count
LA 265	Shortgrass	Early to Middle Coalition	Sherd scatter	1.00	1
LA 266	Shortgrass	Early or Middle Developmental; Coalition	Unknown	1.00	1
LA 272	Shortgrass	Early to Middle Developmental	6 pithouses	4.00	1
LA 327	Shortgrass, Riparian	Late Developmental to Middle Coalition	11 rooms	4.66	1
LA 328	Shortgrass	Middle or Late Developmental to Middle Coalition	20 rooms, 1–3 kivas	6.25	1
LA 329	Shortgrass	Middle or Late Developmental to Middle Coalition	15–25 rooms, 1–3 kivas	4.20	1
LA 330	Shortgrass	Early Coalition to Middle Classic	4–8 rooms, 1 kiva	3.50	1
LA 331	Juniper–Shortgrass	Middle Developmental to Middle Coalition	75 rooms, 12 kivas	22.75	1
LA 332	Shortgrass	Middle Developmental to Middle Coalition	20 rooms, 1 kiva	6.25	1
LA 333	Shortgrass	Early to Middle Coalition	Unknown	1.00	1
LA 369	Shortgrass	Middle to Late Coalition	Sherd scatter	1.00	1
LA 408	Shortgrass	Middle to Late Coalition	Sherd scatter	1.00	1
LA 409	Shortgrass	Middle to Late Coalition	Sherd scatter	1.00	1
LA 1098	Juniper–Shortgrass; Riparian	Historic	1 room	2.00	2

TABLE 5. Continued

Site Number	Lifezone	Phases Present	Estimated Number of Structures	Site Weight	Natural District
LA 1991	Riparian	Historic	Possible tureon	2.00	2
LA 3138	Shortgrass	Early Period	Lithic scatter	1.00	7
LA 4445	Shortgrass	Coalition or Classic; Historic	2 rock-shelters	1.29	2
LA 5102	Juniper-Shortgrass	Early Period	Lithic scatter	1.00	1
LA 5103	Juniper-Shortgrass	Early Period	Lithic scatter	1.00	1
LA 5107	Shortgrass	Early Period	Lithic scatter	1.00	1
LA 5109	Juniper-Shortgrass	Unknown	Petroglyph	—	1
LA 5119	Juniper-Shortgrass	Early Period	Unknown	1.00	1
LA 5141	Shortgrass, Riparian	Unknown	Lithic scatter	—	1
LA 5142	Juniper-Shortgrass	Early Period	Lithic scatter	1.00	1
LA 5143	Juniper-Shortgrass	Early Period	Lithic scatter	1.00	1
LA 5144	Juniper-Shortgrass	Early Period	Lithic scatter	1.00	1
LA 5145	Juniper-Shortgrass	Early Period	Lithic scatter	1.00	1
LA 6169	Shortgrass, Riparian	Late Developmental; Historic	15–20 rooms, 1 kiva, 1 historic structure	17.00 2.00 (his.)	1
LA 6170	Shortgrass, Riparian	Coalition; Historic	10–12 rooms, 1–2 kivas, 2 historic structures	4.66 3.00 (his.)	1

Site	Environment	Period	Description	Value	Components
LA 6171	Shortgrass	Coalition	20–30 rooms, 2–3 kivas	8.33	1
LA 6172	Shortgrass	Early Developmental	3 pithouses	4.00	1
LA 6173	Shortgrass, Riparian	Early Developmental	Sherd and lithic scatter	3.00	1
LA 6174	Shortgrass, Riparian	Early to Middle Developmental	1 pithouse, 1 room	2.00	1
LA 6175	Shortgrass, Riparian	Unknown	2 pithouses, 1 room	Indeterm.	1
LA 6176	Shortgrass, Riparian	Historic	1 room	2.00	1
LA 6177	Piñon-Juniper, Riparian	Coalition	18 rooms, 1 kiva	7.33	1
LA 6178	Piñon-Juniper-Shortgrass Ecotone	Historic	4 rooms within a stockade	1.57	1
LA 6179	Shortgrass	Historic	1 room	2.00	1
LA 6180	Shortgrass	Historic	1 room	2.00	1
LA 6181	Shortgrass	Historic	1 room	2.00	1
LA 6182	Shortgrass	Historic	1 room	2.00	1
LA 6295	Shortgrass	Classic	1 shrine	1.33	2
LA 6296	Unknown	Unknown	Unknown	Indeterm.	2
LA 6297	Shortgrass	Unknown	1 shrine	Indeterm.	2
LA 6455	Shortgrass	Early Coalition to Late Classic	100 rooms, 3 kivas	17.16	1
LA 6456	Shortgrass	Middle Coalition	8 rooms, 1 kiva	10.00	1
LA 6457	Juniper-Shortgrass	Unknown	1 room	Indeterm.	1
LA 6458	Juniper-Shortgrass	Late Coalition to Middle Classic	1 room	1.33	1

TABLE 5. Continued

Site Number	Lifezone	Phases Present	Estimated Number of Structures	Site Weight	Natural District
LA 6459	Juniper–Shortgrass	Unknown	Lithic scatter	Indeterm.	1
LA 6460	Juniper–Shortgrass	Late Coalition to Late Classic	4–6 rooms	1.25	1
LA 6461	Shortgrass	Early Coalition to Early Classic	75 rooms, 1 kiva	20.00	1
LA 6462	Shortgrass	Late Developmental to Early Classic	80–120 rooms, 3–4 kivas	2.60	1
LA 6463	Shortgrass	Late Coalition to Early Classic	2–3 rooms	2.00	1
LA 6464	Shortgrass	Late Coalition to Early Classic	1 room	1.50	1
LA 6793	Shortgrass	Historic	1 room	2.00	1
LA 6981	Juniper–Shortgrass; Riparian Piñon–Juniper	Unknown	Unknown	Indeterm.	2
LA 8720	Shortgrass	Early Period; Early Classic	1 shrine	1.50	1
LA 8993	Shortgrass, Riparian	Late Developmental to Late Coalition; Early or Middle Classic	4 rooms	2.00	2
LA 9063	Shortgrass	Unknown	Petroglyph	Indeterm.	2
LA 9064	Juniper–Shortgrass	Unknown	Petroglyph	Indeterm.	2
LA 9137	Shortgrass	Historic	1 rock-shelter	2.00	1
LA 9139	Shortgrass	Historic	1 room	2.00	1
LA 9140	Shortgrass	Late Developmental	3 pithouses	4.00	1

Site	Vegetation	Cultural Period	Description	Value	
LA 9141	Shortgrass	Historic	1 cave	2.00	1
LA 9154	Shortgrass	Early to Middle Classic	42 rooms, 2 kivas	23.00	1
LA 10102	Shortgrass	Unknown	Petroglyph	Indeterm.	1
LA 10608	Piñon-Juniper	Unknown	1 room	Indeterm.	3
LA 10609	Piñon-Juniper	Middle Developmental; Historic	3 rooms	1.50	3
LA 10610	Piñon-Juniper	Unknown	1 room	Indeterm.	3
LA 10611	Piñon-Juniper–Ponderosa Ecotone	Historic	1 room	2.00	3
LA 10612	Ponderosa, Riparian	Early to Middle Classic	1 room	1.50	3
LA 10613	Shortgrass	Unknown	3 rooms	Indeterm.	5
LA 10614	Shortgrass	Late Developmental	1 room, 1 pithouse	3.00	5
LA 10616	Piñon-Juniper	Unknown	1 enclosure	Indeterm.	4
LA 10617	Piñon-Juniper, Riparian	Early or Middle Classic	1 room	1.50	4
LA 10618	Shortgrass	Unknown	1 shrine	Indeterm.	6
LA 10619	Shortgrass	Unknown	Petroglyph	Indeterm.	6
LA 10621	Piñon-Juniper	Late Developmental or Early Coalition to Early or Middle Classic	3 rock-shelters	1.75	4
LA 10622	Shortgrass	Unknown	1 shrine	Indeterm.	4
LA 10623	Juniper-Shortgrass	Unknown	1 shrine	Indeterm.	4
LA 10624	Shortgrass, Riparian	Historic	8 rock-shelters	9.00	4
LA 10625	Juniper-Shortgrass	Early or Middle Classic	Sherd and lithic scatter	1.00	4

TABLE 5. Continued

Site Number	Lifezone	Phases Present	Estimated Number of Structures	Site Weight	Natural District
LA 10626	Shortgrass	Historic	Trail	1.00	4
LA 10627	Shortgrass	Unknown	1 room	Indeterm.	4
LA 10628	Shortgrass	Historic	1 cairn, 1 room	3.00	4
LA 10629	Juniper-Shortgrass	Unknown	3 shrines	Indeterm.	7
LA 10630	Shortgrass	Unknown	Petroglyph	Indeterm.	7
LA 10645	Shortgrass	Unknown	Petroglyph	Indeterm.	2
LA 10646	Shortgrass	Unknown	Petroglyph	Indeterm.	2
LA 10647	Juniper-Shortgrass	Unknown	Lithic scatter	Indeterm.	2
LA 10648	Riparian	Unknown	Petroglyph	Indeterm.	2
LA 10649	Piñon-Juniper	Historic	Unknown	1.00	3
LA 10650	Juniper-Shortgrass	Unknown	Petroglyph	Indeterm.	2
LA 10651	Juniper-Shortgrass	Historic	1 enclosure	2.00	2
LA 10652	Shortgrass	Unknown	1 shrine	Indeterm.	2
LA 10653	Shortgrass	Unknown	Petroglyph	Indeterm.	2
LA 10654	Juniper-Shortgrass	Late Developmental	Sherd and lithic scatter	1.00	2
LA 10655	Shortgrass	Early or Middle Classic	Sherd and lithic scatter	1.00	6
LA 10656	Shortgrass	Unknown	Petroglyph	Indeterm.	6
LA 10657	Shortgrass	Unknown	Petroglyph	Indeterm.	6
LA 10658	Shortgrass	Unknown	1 room	Indeterm.	6
LA 10659	Shortgrass	Historic	3 rock-shelters	4.00	6

LA 10660	Shortgrass	Unknown	Lithic scatter	Indeterm.	6
LA 10661	Riparian	Unknown	Lithic scatter	Indeterm.	2
LA 10662	Juniper-Shortgrass	Unknown	Lithic scatter	Indeterm.	2
LA 10663	Riparian	Late Developmental; Early or Middle Classic; Historic	2 rooms	1.50	2
LA 10664	Shortgrass	Unknown	Petroglyph	Indeterm.	2
LA 10665	Shortgrass	Unknown	Petroglyph	Indeterm.	2
LA 10666	Riparian	Early Classic; Historic	4 rooms	3.00	2
LA 10667	Juniper-Shortgrass	Unknown	Petroglyph	Indeterm.	2
LA 10668	Shortgrass, Riparian	Early or Middle Classic	2 rooms	2.00	2
LA 10669	Shortgrass, Riparian	Late Developmental; Early or Middle Classic	1 room	1.33	2
LA 10670	Riparian	Unknown	1 room	Indeterm.	2
LA 10671	Piñon-Juniper, Riparian	Early or Middle Classic	1 room	1.50	3
LA 10672	Juniper-Shortgrass	Unknown	Petroglyph	Indeterm.	2
LA 10673	Juniper-Shortgrass	Historic	1 room	2.00	2
LA 10674	Juniper-Shortgrass	Unknown	Petroglyph	Indeterm.	2
LA 10675	Juniper-Shortgrass	Unknown	Petroglyph	Indeterm.	2
LA 10676	Juniper-Shortgrass	Unknown	Petroglyph	Indeterm.	2

TABLE 5. *Continued*

Site Number	Lifezone	Phases Present	Estimated Number of Structures	Site Weight	Natural District
LA 10677	Juniper-Short-grass	Unknown	Petroglyph	Indeterm.	2
LA 10678	Juniper-Short-grass; Riparian	Middle Developmental	4 rooms	5.00	2
LA 10679	Juniper-Short-grass	Unknown	2 rooms	Indeterm.	2
LA 10680	Juniper-Short-grass	Historic	mine	1.00	2
LA 10681	Juniper-Short-grass	Historic	mine	1.00	2
LA 10682	Juniper-Short-grass	Middle Classic	1 room	2.00	2
LA 10683	Shortgrass	Late Developmental	Sherd scatter	1.00	2
LA 10684	Juniper-Short-grass; Riparian	Middle Developmental; Historic	Sherd scatter	1.00	2
LA 10685	Shortgrass	Historic	Sherd and lithic scatter	1.00	2
LA 10686	Juniper-Short-grass	Developmental	Sherd and lithic scatter	1.00	2
LA 10687	Shortgrass	Historic	1 room	2.00	2
LA 10688	Juniper-Short-grass	Historic	1 room	2.00	2
LA 10691	Shortgrass	Unknown	3 rooms	Indeterm.	2
LA 10692	Riparian	Middle Developmental; Historic	2 rooms	2.00	2
LA 10693	Juniper-Short-grass; Riparian	Historic	3 rooms	4.00	2

96

Site	Vegetation	Period	Feature		Number
LA 10694	Juniper-Short-grass; Riparian	Historic	4 rooms	5.00	2
LA 10695	Juniper-Short-grass	Late Developmental	2 rooms	3.00	2
LA 10696	Juniper-Short-grass	Unknown	Petroglyph	Indeterm.	2
LA 10697	Shortgrass	Unknown	1 room	Indeterm.	2
LA 10698	Riparian	Unknown	Petroglyph	Indeterm.	2
LA 10699	Piñon-Juniper	Historic	Mine shaft	1.00	3
LA 10700	Piñon-Juniper–Ponderosa Ecotone	Early Classic	Sherd scatter	1.00	3
LA 10701	Piñon-Juniper	Early to Middle Coalition; Historic	1 possible pithouse	2.00 1.00	3

TABLE 6.
Site Components by Period and Phase in the Study Area

	Developmental Period Early Phase		Developmental Period Middle Phase	
Sites with Early Phase Components	Sites Abandoned Before Beginning of Middle Phase	Sites Remaining Settled into the Middle Phase	Sites Newly Settled During the Middle Phase
LA 55	LA 177	LA 55	LA 150
LA 113	LA 6172	LA 113	LA 247
LA 177	LA 6173	LA 230	LA 256
LA 230		LA 249	LA 328
LA 249		LA 266	LA 329
LA 266		LA 272	LA 331
LA 272		LA 6174	LA 332
LA 6172		LA 10686	LA 10609
LA 6173			LA 10678
LA 6174			LA 10684
LA 10686			LA 10692

	Developmental Period Middle Phase		Developmental Period Late Phase	
Sites with Middle Phase Components	Sites Abandoned Before Beginning of Late Phase	Sites Remaining Settled into the Late Phase	Sites Newly Settled During the Late Phase
LA 55	LA 55	LA 150	LA 327
LA 113	LA 113	LA 247	LA 166
LA 150	LA 230	LA 249	LA 126
LA 230	LA 266	LA 256	LA 148
LA 247	LA 272	LA 328	LA 191
LA 249	LA 6174	LA 329	LA 6169
LA 256	LA 10609	LA 331	LA 6462

Developmental Period Late Phase		Coalition Period Early Phase	
Sites with Late Phase Components	Sites Abandoned Before Beginning of Early Phase	Sites Remaining Settled into the Early Phase	Sites Newly Settled During the Early Phase
LA 266	LA 10678	LA 332	LA 8993
LA 272	LA 10684	LA 10686	LA 9140
LA 328	LA 10692		LA 10614
LA 329			LA 10621
LA 331			LA 10654
LA 126	LA 148	LA 126	LA 3
LA 148	LA 166	LA 150	LA 7
LA 150	LA 191	LA 247	LA 16
LA 166	LA 256	LA 249	LA 70
LA 191	LA 6169	LA 327	LA 76
LA 247	LA 9140	LA 328	LA 113
LA 249	LA 10614	LA 329	LA 265
LA 256	LA 10654	LA 331	LA 266
LA 327	LA 10663	LA 332	LA 330
LA 328	LA 10669	LA 6462	LA 333
LA 329	LA 10683	LA 8993	LA 4445
LA 331	LA 10686	LA 10621	LA 6170
LA 332	LA 10695		LA 6171
LA 6169			LA 6177
LA 6462			LA 6455
LA 8993			LA 6461
LA 9140			LA 10701
LA 10614			
LA 10621			
LA 10654			
LA 10663			
LA 10669			
LA 10683			
LA 10686			
LA 10695			

TABLE 6. Continued

Coalition Period Early Phase		Coalition Period Middle Phase	
Sites with Early Phase Components	Sites Abandoned Before Beginning of Middle Phase	Sites Remaining Settled into the Middle Phase	Sites Newly Settled During the Middle Phase
LA 3	LA 3	LA 7	LA 369
LA 7	LA 13	LA 16	LA 408
LA 16	LA 10621	LA 70	LA 409
LA 70		LA 76	LA 6456
LA 76		LA 126	
LA 113		LA 150	
LA 126		LA 247	
LA 150		LA 249	
LA 247		LA 265	
LA 249		LA 266	
LA 265		LA 327	
LA 266		LA 328	
LA 327		LA 329	
LA 328		LA 330	
LA 329		LA 331	
LA 330		LA 332	
LA 331		LA 333	
LA 332		LA 4445	
LA 333		LA 6170	
LA 4445		LA 6171	
LA 6170		LA 6177	
LA 6171		LA 6455	
LA 6177		LA 6461	
LA 6455		LA 6462	
LA 6461		LA 8993	
LA 6462		LA 10701	
LA 8993			
LA 10621			
LA 10701			

	Coalition Period Middle Phase		Coalition Period Late Phase	
	Sites with Middle Phase Components	Sites Abandoned Before Beginning of Late Phase	Sites Remaining Settled into the Late Phase	Sites Newly Settled During the Late Phase
	LA 7	LA 247	LA 7	LA 12
	LA 16	LA 265	LA16	LA 149
	LA 70	LA 327	LA 70	LA 6458
	LA 76	LA 328	LA 76	LA 6460
	LA 126	LA 329	LA 126	LA 6463
	LA 150	LA 330	LA 150	LA 6464
	LA 247	LA 331	LA 249	
	LA 249	LA 332	LA 266	
	LA 265	LA 333	LA 369	
	LA 266	LA 6456	LA 408	
	LA 327	LA 10701	LA 409	
	LA 328		LA 4445	
	LA 329		LA 6170	
	LA 330		LA 6171	
	LA 331		LA 6177	
	LA 332		LA 6455	
	LA 333		LA 6461	
	LA 369		LA 6462	
	LA 408		LA 8993	
	LA 409			
	LA 4445			
	LA 6170			
	LA 6171			
	LA 6177			
	LA 6455			
	LA 6456			
	LA 6461			
	LA 6462			
	LA 8993			
	LA 10701			

TABLE 6. Continued

| | Coalition Period Late Phase | | Classic Period Early Phase |
Sites with Late Phase Components	Sites Abandoned Before Beginning of Early Phase	Sites Remaining Settled into the Early Phase	Sites Newly Settled During the Early Phase
LA 7	LA 76	LA 7	LA 6295
LA 12	LA 150	LA 12	LA 8720
LA 16	LA 266	LA 16	LA 9154
LA 70	LA 369	LA 70	LA 10612
LA 76	LA 408	LA 126	LA 10617
LA 126	LA 409	LA 149	LA 16021
LA 149	LA 6170	LA 249	LA 10625
LA 150	LA 6171	LA 4445	LA 10655
LA 249	LA 6177	LA 6455	LA 10663
LA 266		LA 6458	LA 10666
LA 369		LA 6460	LA 10668
LA 408		LA 6461	LA 10669
LA 409		LA 6462	LA 10671
LA 4445		LA 6463	LA 10700
LA 6170		LA 6464	
LA 6171		LA 8993	
LA 6177			
LA 6455			
LA 6458			
LA 6460			
LA 6461			
LA 6462			
LA 6463			
LA 6464			
LA 8993			

Classic Period Early Phase		Classic Period Middle Phase	
Sites with Early Phase Components	Sites Abandoned Before Beginning of Middle Phase	Sites Remaining Settled into the Middle Phase	Sites Newly Settled During the Middle Phase
LA 7	LA 149	LA 7	LA 5
LA 12	LA 6461	LA 12	LA 164
LA 16	LA 6462	LA 16	LA 10682
LA 70	LA 6463	LA 70	
LA 126	LA 6464	LA 126	
LA 149	LA 8720	LA 249	
LA 249	LA 10666	LA 4445	
LA 4445	LA 10700	LA 6295	
LA 6295		LA 6455	
LA 6455		LA 6458	
LA 6458		LA 6460	
LA 6460		LA 8993	
LA 6461		LA 9154	
LA 6462		LA 10612	
LA 6463		LA 10617	
LA 6464		LA 10621	
LA 8720		LA 10625	
LA 8993		LA 10655	
LA 9154		LA 10663	
LA 10612		LA 10668	
LA 10617		LA 10669	
LA 10621		LA 10671	
LA 10625			
LA 10655			
LA 10663			
LA 10666			
LA 10668			
LA 10669			
LA 10671			
LA 10700			

TABLE 6. Continued

	Classic Period Middle Phase		Classic Period Late Phase	
Sites with Middle Phase Components	Sites Abandoned Before Beginning of Late Phase	Sites Remaining Settled into the Late Phase	Sites Newly Settled During the Late Phase
LA 5	LA 5	LA 7	LA 165
LA 7	LA 12	LA 70	
LA 12	LA 16	LA 126	
LA 16	LA 164	LA 249	
LA 70	LA 6458	LA 4445	
LA 126	LA 8993	LA 6295	
LA 164	LA 9154	LA 6455	
LA 249	LA 10612	LA 6460	
LA 4445	LA 10617		
LA 6295	LA 10621		
LA 6455	LA 10625		
LA 6458	LA 10655		
LA 6460	LA 10663		
LA 8993	LA 10668		
LA 9154	LA 10669		
LA 10612	LA 10671		
LA 10617	LA 10682		
LA 10621			
LA 16025			
LA 10655			
LA 10663			
LA 10668			
LA 10669			
LA 10671			
LA 10682			

	Classic Period Late Phase		Historic Period	
Sites with Late Phase Components	Sites Abandoned Before Beginning of Historic Period	Sites Remaining Settled into the Historic Period	Sites Newly Settled During the Historic Period	
LA 7	LA 7	LA 126	LA 16	LA 10611
LA 70	LA 70	LA 165	LA 34	LA 10624
LA 126	LA 249	LA 4445	LA 44	LA 10626
LA 165	LA 6295		LA 115	LA 10628
LA 249	LA 6455		LA 163	LA 10649
LA 4445	LA 6460		LA 164	LA 10651
LA 6295			LA 230	LA 10659
LA 6455			LA 1098	LA 10663
LA 6460			LA 1991	LA 10666
			LA 6169	LA 10673
			LA 6170	LA 10680
			LA 6176	LA 10681
			LA 6178	LA 10684
			LA 6179	LA 10685
			LA 6180	LA 10687
			LA 6181	LA 10688
			LA 6182	LA 10692
			LA 6793	LA 10693
			LA 9137	LA 10694
			LA 9139	LA 10699
			LA 9141	LA 10701
			LA 10609	

TABLE 7.
Site Components by Period and Phase in the Six Natural Districts in the Study Area

1. *Rio Grande Floodplain and Terraces Natural District*

Developmental Period			Coalition Period		
Early Phase	Middle Phase	Late Phase	Early Phase	Middle Phase	Late Phase
LA 55	LA 55	LA 126	LA 70	LA 70	LA 70
LA 113	LA 113	LA 247	LA 113	LA 126	LA 126
LA 249	LA 247	LA 249	LA 126	LA 247	LA 249
LA 266	LA 249	LA 327	LA 247	LA 249	LA 266
LA 272	LA 266	LA 328	LA 249	LA 265	LA 369
LA 6172	LA 272	LA 329	LA 265	LA 266	LA 408
LA 6173	LA 328	LA 331	LA 266	LA 327	LA 409
LA 6174	LA 329	LA 332	LA 327	LA 328	LA 6170
	LA 331	LA 6169	LA 328	LA 329	LA 6171
	LA 332	LA 6462	LA 329	LA 330	LA 6177
	LA 6174	LA 9140	LA 330	LA 331	LA 6455
			LA 331	LA 332	LA 6458
			LA 332	LA 333	LA 6460
			LA 333	LA 369	LA 6461
			LA 6170	LA 408	LA 6462
			LA 6171	LA 409	LA 6463
			LA 6177	LA 6170	LA 6464
			LA 6455	LA 6171	
			LA 6461	LA 6177	
			LA 6462	LA 6455	
				LA 6456	
				LA 6461	
				LA 6462	

	Classic Period		Historic Period
Early Phase	Middle Phase	Late Phase	
LA 70	LA 70	LA 70	LA 34
LA 126	LA 126	LA 126	LA 126
LA 249	LA 249	LA 249	LA 6169
LA 6455	LA 6455	LA 6455	LA 6170
LA 6458	LA 6458	LA 6460	LA 6176
LA 6460	LA 6460		LA 6178
LA 6461	LA 9154		LA 6179
LA 6462			LA 6180
LA 6463			LA 6181
LA 6464			LA 6182
LA 8720			LA 6793
LA 9154			LA 9137
			LA 9139
			LA 9141

2. *Santa Fe River Canyon Natural District*

	Developmental Period			Coalition Period	
Early Phase	Middle Phase	Late Phase	Early Phase	Middle Phase	Late Phase
LA 177	LA 150	LA 148	LA 3	LA 7	LA 7
LA 230	LA 230	LA 150	LA 7	LA 16	LA 16
LA 10686	LA 256	LA 166	LA 16	LA 150	LA 149
	LA 10678	LA 256	LA 150	LA 4445	LA 150
	LA 10684	LA 8993	LA 4445	LA 8993	LA 4445
	LA 18686	LA 10654	LA 8993		LA 8993
	LA 18692	LA 10663			
		LA 10669			
		LA 10683			
		LA 10686			
		LA 10695			

TABLE 7. Continued

	Classic Period		Historic Period	
Early Phase	Middle Phase	Late Phase		
LA 7	LA 7	LA 7	LA 16	LA 10666
LA 16	LA 16	LA 165	LA 44	LA 10673
LA 149	LA 164	LA 4445	LA 115	LA 10680
LA 4445	LA 4445	LA 6295	LA 163	LA 10681
LA 6295	LA 6295		LA 164	LA 10684
LA 8993	LA 8993		LA 165	LA 10685
LA 10663	LA 10663		LA 230	LA 10687
LA 10666	LA 10668		LA 1098	LA 10688
LA 10668	LA 10669		LA 1991	LA 10692
LA 10669	LA 10671		LA 4445	LA 10693
LA 10671	LA 10682		LA 10651	LA 10694
			LA 10663	

3. Upper Arroyo Hondo Natural District

Developmental Period			Coalition Period		
Early Phase	Middle Phase	Late Phase	Early Phase	Middle Phase	Late Phase
None known	LA 10609	None known	LA 76	LA 76	LA 12
			LA 10701	LA 10701	LA 76

Classic Period			Historic Period
Early Phase	Middle Phase	Late Phase	
LA 12	LA 12	None known	LA 10609
LA 10612			LA 10611
LA 10700			LA 10649
			LA 10699
			LA 10701

4. Tetilla Canyon Natural District

Developmental Period

Early Phase	Middle Phase	Late Phase
None known	None known	LA 10621

Coalition Period

Early Phase	Middle Phase	Late Phase
LA 10621	None known	None known

Classic Period

Early Phase	Middle Phase	Late Phase
LA 10617	LA 5	None known
LA 10621	LA 10617	
LA 10625	LA 10621	
	LA 10625	

Historic Period

Early Phase	Middle Phase	Late Phase
	LA 10624	
	LA 10626	
	LA 10628	

5. Middle Arroyo Hondo Natural District

Developmental Period

Early Phase	Middle Phase	Late Phase
None known	None known	LA 191
		LA 10614

Coalition Period

Early Phase	Middle Phase	Late Phase
None known	None known	None known

Classic Period

Early Phase	Middle Phase	Late Phase
None known	None known	None known

Historic Period

Early Phase	Middle Phase	Late Phase
None known	None known	None known

6. The Canyon at the Edge of La Bajada Mesa Natural District

Developmental Period

Early Phase	Middle Phase	Late Phase
None known	None known	None known

Coalition Period

Early Phase	Middle Phase	Late Phase
None known	None known	None known

Classic Period

Early Phase	Middle Phase	Late Phase
LA 10655	LA 10655	None known

Historic Period

Early Phase	Middle Phase	Late Phase
	LA 10659	

Appendix C

CERAMIC INVENTORY FROM THE ARROYO HONDO ARCHAEOLOGICAL SURVEY

The ceramics collected during the Arroyo Hondo site survey were identified by Richard W. Lang in 1971. The following list gives the number of sherds of each type or other category collected at each site where surface material was found.

SITE LA 3

Kwahe'e B/W	6
Santa Fe B/W	81
Galisteo B/W	1
Unidentified B/W	12
St. Johns Poly	1
Plain Gray	6
Unindented Corrugated	3
Tooled Unindented Corrugated	1
Smeared Unindented Corrugated	1
Indented Corrugated	1
Tesuque Smeared Indented	16

SITE LA 5

Abiquiu B/G	2
Bandelier B/G	10

Agua Fria G/R	15
Unidentified G/R	27
Cieneguilla G/Y	14
Largo G/Y	11
Sanchez G/Y	3
Unidentified G/Y	46
Largo G/Poly	10
Sanchez G/Poly	3
San Clemente G/Poly	18
Espinosa G/Poly	4
Unidentified G/Poly	3
Plain Gray	5
Tesuque Smeared Indented	1

SITE LA 8

Escavada B/W	1
Santa Fe B/W	2
Unidentified B/W	1
Plain Gray	3

111

Smeared Unindented Corrugated	1
Tesuque Smeared Indented	4

SITE LA 16

Mesa Verde B/W	1
Kwahe'e B/W	1
Santa Fe B/W	36
Vallecitos B/W	3
Galisteo B/W	13
Poge B/W	30
Pindi B/W	7
Wiyo B/W	22
Abiquiu B/G	36
Bandelier B/G	21
Sankawi B/C?	3
Tewa Poly	8
Tewa-Ogapoge Poly	1
Pojoaque Poly	5
Ogapoge Poly	3
Powhoge Poly	7
Kiua Poly	5
Unidentified Matte Paint Poly	33
St. Johns Poly	1
Agua Fria G/R	56
Rayo G/R	1
Largo G/R	2
Sanchez G/R	1
Unidentified G/R	180
Cieneguilla G/Y	100
Largo G/Y	55
Sanchez G/Y	7
Unidentified G/Y	274
Arenal G/Poly	2
Cieneguilla G/Poly	6
Largo G/Poly	9
Cieneguilla or Largo G/Poly	10
Sanchez G/Poly	1
San Clemente G/Poly	116
Espinosa G/Poly	11
Unidentified G/Poly	4
Plain Brown	1
Plain Gray	27
Scored or Brushed	1
Unindented Corrugated	2
Indented Corrugated	8
Tesuque Smeared Indented	14
Cordova Micaceous Ribbed	1
Plain Micaceous-Slipped	2
Polished Brown	2
Polished Red	7

Posuge Red	12
Polished Black	17
Kapo Black	4
San Ildefonso Black	1
Glass (Clear)	1
Non-Indian Earthenware	3
Non-Indian China or Stoneware	19

SITE LA 76

Kwahe'e B/W	1
Santa Fe B/W	36
Socorro B/W	2
Galisteo B/W	2
Poge B/W	16
Pindi	3
Agua Fria G/R	1
Plain Brown	1
Plain Gray	25
Unindented Corrugated	4
Indented Corrugated	2
Tesuque Smeared Indented	73
Cordova Micaceous Ribbed	1
Kapo Black	2

SITE LA 148

Red Mesa B/W	12
Escavada B/W	4
Unidentified B/W	10
Plain Gray	6
Unindented Corrugated	1
Smeared Unindented Corrugated	1
Non-Indian China or Stoneware	1

SITE LA 164

Tewa Poly	5
Puname Poly	5
Unidentified Matte Paint Poly	9
Agua Fria G/R	1
Kotyiti G/R	2
Largo G/Y	1
Kotyiti G/Y	3
Unidentified G/Y	1
Plain Gray	8
Polished Brown	18
Polished Red	9
Posuge Red	7
Kapo Black	16

SITE LA 166

Red Mesa B/W	62

112

Escavada B/W	10
Unidentified B/W	63
San Clemente G/Poly	2
Plain Brown	5
Plain Gray	36
Scored or Brushed	3
Unindented Corrugated	7
Tooled Unindented Corrugated	6
Smeared Unindented Corrugated	10

SITE LA 191

Escavada B/W	18
Gallup B/W	7
Chaco B/W	1
McElmo B/W	1
Kwahe'e B/W	18
Santa Fe B/W	12
Socorro B/W	23
Wingate or Puerco B/R	1
Plain Brown	1
Plain Gray	24
Scored or Brushed	1
Taos Incised	1
Unindented Corrugated	1
Smeared Unindented Corrugated	1
Indented Corrugated	54
Smeared Indented Corrugated	1

SITE LA 235

Unidentified Matte Paint Poly	1
Non-Indian Earthenware	6
Non-Indian China or Stoneware	1

SITE LA 1991

Unidentified Matte Paint Poly	1
Kapo Black	1

SITE LA 4445

Tewa Poly	1
Unidentified Matte Paint Poly	1
Tesuque Smeared Indented	6
Polished Red	1
Posuge Red	3

SITE LA 6295

Unidentified G/Y	1

SITE LA 8993

Kwahe'e B/W	12
Santa Fe B/W	48
Socorro B/W	2

Unidentified B/W	4
Agua Fria G/R	1
Unidentified G/Y	3
Plain Gray	11
Unindented Corrugated	1
Smeared Unindented Corrugated	2
Indented Corrugated	1
Tesuque Smeared Indented	47

SITE LA 10608

Plain Gray	1

SITE LA 10609

Red Mesa B/W	1
Tewa Poly	2
Unidentified Matte Paint Poly	3
Polished Brown	1
Polished Red	7
Posuge Red	1
Kapo Black	3

SITE LA 10611

Plain Gray	2
Polished Black	9

SITE LA 10612

Agua Fria B/R	2

SITE LA 10613

Escavada B/W	4
Kwahe'e B/W	1
Santa Fe B/W	2
Socorro B/W	2
Unidentified B/W	1
Plain Gray	24
Unindented Corrugated	1
Smeared Unindented Corrugated	1
Indented Corrugated	12

SITE LA 10614

Unidentified Rio Grande Glaze?	1
Plain Gray	13
Indented Corrugated	8
Tesuque Smeared Indented	3

SITE LA 10617

Unidentified G/Y	1

SITE LA 10620

Bandelier B/G	1
Agua Fria G/R	1
Unidentified G/Y	8

113

SITE LA 10621
Unidentified B/W   1
Abiquiu B/G   1
Unidentified G/R   3
Unidentified G/Y   1
Largo G/Poly   2
San Clemente G/Poly   1
Plain Gray   2
Tesuque Smeared Indented   2

SITE LA 10624
Unidentified Matte Paint Poly   1

SITE LA 10625
Agua Fria G/R   18

SITE LA 10626
Polished Red   1
Polished Black   1

SITE LA 10628
Unidentified Matte Paint Poly   1
Glass   1

SITE LA 10651
Polished Brown   1
Polished Red   1

SITE LA 10653
Plain Gray   2

SITE LA 10654
Escavada B/W   4
Unidentified B/W   3
Smeared Unindented Corrugated   1

SITE LA 10655
Agua Fria G/R   2
Unidentified G/Y   7
San Clemente G/Poly   3
Tesuque Smeared Indented   2

SITE LA 10659
Kapo Black   2

SITE LA 10662
Polished Brown   1

SITE LA 10663
Santa Fe B/W   33
Unidentified B/W   6

Unidentified Matte Paint Poly   3
Unidentified G/Y   2
Plain Gray   1
Smeared Unindented Corrugated   1
Tesuque Smeared Indented   3
Non-Indian China or Stoneware   1

SITE LA 10666
Tewa Poly   10
Pojoaque Poly   4
Ogapoge Poly   3
Powhoge Poly   2
Puname Poly   6
Unidentified Matte Paint Poly   108
Unidentified G/Y   4
San Clemente G/Poly   3
Plain Gray   71
Scored or Brushed   4
Plain Micaceous-Slipped   5
Polished Brown   34
Polished Red   29
Polished Black   51
Kapo Black   1

SITE LA 10668
Galisteo B/W   1
Agua Fria G/R   3
Tesuque Smeared Indented   3

SITE LA 10669
Escavada B/W   1
Kwahe'e B/W   2
Santa Fe B/W   1
Unidentified B/W   1
Cieneguilla G/Y   1
Plain Gray   2

SITE LA 10670
Santa Fe B/W   3

SITE LA 10671
Unidentified G/Poly   1

SITE LA 10673
Unidentified Matte Paint Poly   1
Polished Brown   6

SITE LA 10678
Red Mesa B/W   8
Unidentified G/R   1

114

Plain Gray   2
Unindented Corrugated   3

SITE LA 10679
Unidentified G/R   1

SITE LA 10682
Agua Fria G/R   8
Largo G/Y   2
Unidentified G/Y   1
Plain Gray   4

SITE LA 10683
Escavada B/W   2
Kwahe'e B/W   11
Galisteo B/W   1
Plain Gray   24
Scored or Brushed   5
Indented Corrugated   39

SITE LA 10684
Red Mesa B/W   1
Unidentified Matte Paint Poly   8
Plain Brown   12
Polished Brown   11
Polished Red   6
Polished Black   14

SITE LA 10685
Pojoaque Poly   2
Powhoge Poly   4
Puname Poly   5
Zia Poly   2
Unidentified Matte Paint Poly   57
Plain Gray   25
Polished Brown   19
Polished Red   9
Polished Black   35
Non-Indian China or Stoneware   1

SITE LA 10686
Unidentified B/W   1

SITE LA 10687
Non-Indian China or Stoneware   1

SITE LA 10692
Red Mesa B/W   1
Unidentified Matte Paint Poly   8

Plain Gray   5
Polished Red   1
Glass   3
Non-Indian China or Stoneware   10

SITE LA 10693
Kiua Poly   2
Unidentified Matte Paint Poly   2
Plain Gray   2
Polished Black   2
Glass   70
Non-Indian China or Stoneware   25

SITE LA 10695
Santa Fe B/W   2
Unidentified B/W   2
Tesuque Smeared Indented   5

SITE LA 10699
Polished Black   1

SITE LA 10700
San Clemente G/Poly   25

115

Appendix D

SITES IMMEDIATELY BEYOND THE SUSTAINING AREA AND TRANSECT

SITES IMMEDIATELY SOUTH OF THE SUSTAINING AREA

Site LA 4 (Chamisa Locita)

This site consists of five major mounds, representing at least 16 roomblocks, and one circular depression. It is located north of Highway 285 and west of that highway's junction with Interstate 25 at a point shown on the USGS Seton Village Quadrangle map as Pueblo Well. Chamisa Locita lies in a basin formed by the channels of two major arroyos and several minor ones. It is slightly above the northern bank of the southeastern tributary of Cañon Ancha and is bordered on the north, east, and south by the westernmost foothills of the Sangre de Cristo Mountains. To the west of the site, Cañon Ancha forms a gap in the foothills leading onto the Rio Grande piedmont. The lifezone here is piñon-juniper woodland.

Chamisa Locita was excavated by Nels Nelson in 1914 and test pitted for tree-ring specimens by W. S. Stallings sometime between 1932 and 1937. Neither individual published accounts of the site, but Nelson's rather brief field notes and sketch map are on file at the

117

Laboratory of Anthropology. According to these notes, LA 4 consists of a long, straight mound with four other roomblocks abutting it perpendicularly. Four additional mounds or roomblock clusters are located between the major mound and the arroyo channel. Nelson apparently dug 44 rooms at the site, excavating between 1 and 5 rooms in 15 of the 16 roomblocks. These rooms were roughly square to rectangular with floors and walls of adobe. The walls of at least one room retained clear evidence of having been decorated with a "fresco in red paint [with] heavy straight lines and thin zigzag." The circular depression, presumably a kiva, shown at the bottom of Nelson's sketch map apparently was not excavated in 1914. The scale of the site shown on Nelson's map suggests that there were between 280 and 300 rooms at the site.

The various sources that deal with the ceramic assemblage from LA 4 are not in complete agreement. According to Smiley, Stubbs, and Bannister (1953:15), the following types were found:

"Indigenous"
  Santa Fe Black-on-white, A.D. 1200–1350
  Wiyo Black-on-white, 1300–1400
  Pindi Black-on-white, 1300–1350
  Galisteo Black-on-white, 1300–1400+
  Poge Black-on-white, 1325–1350
"Trade"
  Rio Grande Glaze I Red, 1300–1390+.

The site card on file for LA 4 at the Laboratory of Anthropology omits Pindi Black-on-white and Poge Black-on-white but lists "indented, micaceous and smeared" culinary ("coil") ware and adds Arenal Glaze Polychrome. Under the title of "Variations or Trade" are included:

  Wiyo Black-on-white, A.D. 1300–1400
  Galisteo Black-on-white, flared rim
  textile impressed.

These ceramic data place the occupation of LA 4 between A.D. 1200 and 1400+. However, five tree-ring dates obtained from pothunters' debris on one mound at the site and reported in Smiley, Stubbs, and Bannister (1953:15) are as follows: "1313C, two at 1321 (1B and 1C), 1330, 1333." The clustering in these dates may indicate a far shorter occupation span at LA 4, perhaps ending before A.D. 1350.

Site LA 8 (Los Alamos or Pueblo Alamo)

This site comprised four mounds containing four more or less contiguous adobe roomblocks on the north side of Highway 285 at its junction with Interstate 25 (the "Lamy cutoff"). The site was located near the head of Cañada de los Alamos in the gap formed by the arroyo in the westernmost foothills of the Sangre de Cristo Mountains. During the summer of 1971, when Interstate 25 and the Highway 285 exit were widened, LA 8 was almost totally destroyed—fortunately, however, not before salvage operations could be performed by the Laboratory of Anthropology.

Like nearby Chamisa Locita (LA 4), LA 8 was first excavated by Nels Nelson in 1914 and then test pitted for tree-ring specimens by W. S. Stallings sometime between 1932 and 1937. Again, Nelson's field notes and map are on file at the Laboratory of Anthropology. The site was dug for the third and final time by Joseph Allen of the Laboratory of Anthropology in the summer of 1971, prior to its destruction by road building activity.

According to Nelson, LA 8 consisted of four mounds with a roomblock in each. On the basis of his map, the site appears to have consisted of about 70 rooms, of which he excavated 24. Allen, who also was only able to excavate a portion of the site, states that it had more than 100 rooms. Both excavators found the rooms to be made of adobe and square to rectangular in shape.

As in the cases of many other known sites revisited during the 1971 Arroyo Hondo survey, the various sources that deal with the ceramic assemblage at LA 8 are not in complete agreement with one another. According to Smiley, Stubbs, and Bannister (1953:17), the categories are as follows:

"Indigenous"
Santa Fe Black-on-white, A.D. 1200–1350
Pindi Black-on-white, 1300–1350
Wiyo Black-on-white, 1300–1400
Galisteo Black-on-white, 1300–1400+
"Trade"
St. John's Polychrome, 1175–1300
Chupadero Black-on-white, 1250–1300.

The site card for LA 8 on file at the Laboratory of Anthropology omits Pindi Black-on-white but lists "plain, ribbed, indented,

119

smeared" culinary ("coil") ware. Under the title of "Variations or Trade" are included:

Wiyo Black-on-white, A.D. 1300–1400
Chupadero Black-on-white, 1250–1300
St. John's Polychrome, 1175–1300
Black-on-white textile impressed
Black-on-white interior, coiled exterior
Black-on-white paste (sic)—polished black interior
rubbed coil, polished black interior.

EVIDENCE OF SITES LOCATED UNDER THE CITY OF SANTA FE

The historic and modern city of Santa Fe is located at the western foot of the Sangre de Cristo Mountains, 7,000 feet above sea level. It is situated in a natural basin formed by the confluences of some 10 major intermittent streams and numerous minor ones with the perennially flowing Santa Fe River. Because this location attracted Spanish settlement as early as A.D. 1609, most of the evidence of prehistoric settlement within the present city limits has long since been obliterated. Traditionally, the city is said to have been founded on top of the long-abandoned ruins of an Indian pueblo called Ogapoge.

The chief source of archaeological data about settlement in the vicinity of Santa Fe comes from sherd collections gathered incidentally during foundation excavations and reported to the Laboratory of Anthropology. These sherd collections seem to fall roughly into five groups:

1. Early black-on-white sherds
2. Late black-on-white sherds
3. Late black-on-white with glaze sherds
4. Late black-on-white with Tewa series sherds
5. Purely Historic sherds.

Seven sherd collections from "sites" fall within the first group of early black-on-white types. The earliest type reported is Red Mesa Black-on-white, dated by Breternitz (1966) between A.D. 850 and A.D. 1125, and the latest is Wiyo Black-on-white, dated by the same author between A.D. 1300 and A.D. 1400 (1966:90,104). Wiyo is found, however, in only one of these collections; if we discount it for the moment, the latest type is Santa Fe Black-on-white, which dates between about A.D. 1200 and A.D. 1350 (Breternitz 1966:95). Red Mesa, Kwahe'e, and Santa Fe Black-on-white are three types common to most of the sites in the first group. Other types found in the various collections in addition to, or instead of, these three are listed below with the numbers of sites in this first group:

LA 111: the three main types only;
LA 114: Chaco II in addition to the three main types;
LA 341: Red Mesa and Chaco II but no Kwahe'e and Santa Fe;
LA 608: Wiyo, Santa Fe, and Red Mesa but no Kwahe'e;
LA 616: Chaco II, Red Mesa, and Kwahe'e but no Santa Fe;
LA 618: the three main types only;
LA 4450-111: Red Mesa, Escavada, and Gallup but no Kwahe'e and Santa Fe.

The second group of collections includes only black-on-white sherds from the later end of the Rio Grande ceramic sequence. The earliest member in these collection is Santa Fe Black-on-white and the latest members are Galisteo and Wiyo Black-on-white. These last two types are dated by Breternitz to between A.D. 1300 and about A.D. 1400 (1966:76,104). Two sites fall in this grouping:

LA 109: Santa Fe and Wiyo Black-on-white;
LA 1876: Santa Fe, Wiyo, and Galisteo Black-on-white.

The third group of collections includes sherds of both the later black-on-white series and Rio Grande glaze wares. The earliest type found in this grouping is Santa Fe Black-on-white, while the latest is Biscuit A, which is dated by Breternitz to between A.D. 1375 and A.D. 1450 (1966:70). Some of the later Rio Grande glaze types, which postdate Biscuit A, may in fact be present in these collections; however, only a Glaze A type is specifically identified in the Laboratory records. Presumably this lack of specific identification is due to an absence of glaze rim sherds, an absence that may reflect the presence of only small amounts of glaze pottery in the collection. The two sites that fall in this group with the types present in each are:

LA 1051: Biscuit A and Rio Grande Glaze Polychrome (sic);
LA 1890: Santa Fe, Wiyo, and Galisteo Black-on-white; Agua Fria Glaze Polychrome.

The fourth group of collections seems to have been drawn from sites having two temporal components. These sites contain both prehistoric black-on-white sherds of either the Santa Fe or Wiyo type and sherds drawn predominantly from the Historic Tewa series. Only one of these sites, LA 1111, contains glaze sherds as well. Four sites fall in this class:

LA 167: Santa Fe Black-on-white and Tewa Polychrome, Tewa Red, and Kotyiti Glaze Polychrome;

LA 179: Santa Fe Black-on-white and Tewa Polychrome, Tewa Polished Red, and Tewa (Kapo) Black;

LA 930: Wiyo Black-on-white and Tewa Polychrome, Tewa Polished Red, Tewa Red-on-black, Tewa White-on-red, Tsia Polychrome, Sankawi Black-on-cream, Kotyiti Glaze Polychrome, and European;

LA 1111: Santa Fe Black-on-white and Rio Grande Glaze Polychrome, Tewa Polychrome, Tewa Polished Red, and Tewa (Kapo) Black.

The final group of sherd collections from Santa Fe includes four sites that contain only Historic sherds. The site numbers and the ceramic types present at each site are listed below:

LA 1522: Tewa Polychrome, Tewa Polished Red, and Tsia Polychrome;

LA 1838: Tewa Polychrome, Tewa Polished Black, and European;

LA 4449: Late culinary (sic), Picuris (sic);

LA 8676: Powhoge Polychrome.

Obviously, this list does not exhaust all the known Historic locations in Santa Fe but instead is merely a compilation of all the sites listed in the Laboratory of Anthropology files that have yielded collections of Historic Indian pottery. Although it cannot be determined whether or not these sherds represent Indian occupation of the area or merely Spanish use of Indian-made pottery, the latter explanation seems most likely.

One other site, LA 4451, could not be grouped in the above categories due to lack of information. Although the site card stated that Rio Grande Glaze Ware was found on the site, the other type present was listed merely as "Tabria" and did not specify whether the black-on-white or polychrome variety was present.

In summary, although ceramic evidence from the modern city of Santa Fe is spotty at best, it seems certain that the upper Santa Fe River valley was occupied by the Middle Phase of the Developmental Period. The presence of Red Mesa Black-on-white sherds seems to place this initial known occupation somewhere in the ninth or tenth century. Further, if the distribution of sherd collections containing only early black-on-white ceramic types can be taken as a fair guide, early settlement clustered within a triangular area centered on the Plaza of modern Santa Fe and bordered on the south and west about one-half mile in each direction by the Santa Fe River and Arroyo Barranca respectively.

In contrast to the black-on-white ceramic sequence, which is well represented in the Santa Fe area, the Rio Grande glaze wares, which overlap and follow them in time, have a markedly lower incidence. Most references to glaze ware in the collections recorded by the Laboratory fail to specify classification beyond the simple generic terms "glaze" or "glaze polychrome." Presumably this failure is due to an absence of rims implying that a low overall quantity of glaze ware occurred in the various collections reported. Of course, this apparent underrepresentation may be the result of sampling error stemming from the haphazard nature of the recovery of sherds. On the other hand, such a lack may very well indicate a depopulation or abandonment of the Santa Fe area prior to the time of the glaze ware ascendency in the Rio Grande. Such an interpretation is further strengthened by the fourth grouping of sherd collections from Santa Fe, which contain both late black-on-white series sherds and Historic wares but lack the intervening biscuit and glaze wares.

There is an apparent occupational hiatus at Arroyo Hondo Pueblo during the middle of the fourteenth century, and settlement seems to have terminated altogether at nearby sites such as Los Alamos (LA 8) to the south and Pindi Pueblo (LA 1) to the west at about the same time. Further, most of the area at the foot of the Sangre de Cristo range surrounding Santa Fe seems to have been empty after the close of the fourteenth century. This information, taken with the apparent interruption in the ceramic sequence beneath the modern city, seems to point to a Classic Period abandonment of the Santa Fe area with major reoccupation coming only with the Spaniards and the onset of Historic times.

SITES CLUSTERED IN THE VICINITY OF AGUA FRIA

The modern town of Agua Fria is located on the south bank of the Santa Fe River slightly over 1½ miles west of the city limits of Santa Fe and about 5 miles northwest of Arroyo Hondo Pueblo. The area around Agua Fria appears to have been an important prehistoric population center but unlike the case of the city of Santa Fe, evidence here was not destroyed by recent construction before it could be investigated scientifically. Around the turn of the twentieth century, A. V. Kidder collected sherds from the surface of LA 2, which he called the "Agua Fria School House" site, and designated it the type site for a red ware that became known to later students as Agua Fria Glaze Red (Kidder 1915:447–50). Stallings worked in the vicinity of Agua Fria and tested LA 2 for tree-ring specimens in the 1930s, and it was during this period that he and Stanley Stubbs of the Laboratory of Anthropology excavated nearby LA 1, Pindi Pueblo (Stubbs and Stallings 1953).

In light of the detailed excavation report published by Stubbs and Stallings on Pindi Pueblo and the almost total lack of information on the other sites reported from the Agua Fria vicinity (except for lists of the ceramic types that occur on their surfaces), no detailed discussion of the archaeology of the Agua Fria area will be presented here. It is sufficient for our purposes to note that, on the basis of the recorded ceramic inventories, sites in the immediate vicinity of Agua Fria fall into two general categories. The first group consists of six sites with the earliest ceramic type reported being Chaco II and the latest Biscuit A. Following Breternitz (1966:70–71), these types would indicate an occupational span between about A.D. 850 and A.D. 1450. The sites in this group are as follows:

LA 1 (Pindi): Chaco II, Kwahe'e, Pindi, Poge, Mesa Verde, Chupadero, Tularosa Black-on-white; St. John's, Springerville, Heshotauthla Polychrome; Rio Grande Glaze I;

LA 2 (School House): Biscuit A Black-on-white; Agua Fria Glaze Red;

LA 117: Santa Fe Black-on-white; Agua Fria Glaze Red;

LA 118: Santa Fe Black-on-white; Agua Fria Glaze Red; San Clemente Glaze Polychrome;

LA 119: Santa Fe Black-on-white; Agua Fria Glaze Red;

LA 1378: Chaco II, Santa Fe Black-on-white.

The second group of sites in the Agua Fria area exhibits essentially Historic ceramic components. Two sites belong to this class, and with the exception of some Red Mesa Black-on-white material recorded at LA 844, all types represent a post-1550 occupation:

LA 844: Red Mesa Black-on-white; Tewa Polychrome, Tewa Polished Red, Tewa (Kapo) Polished Black, Tsia Polychrome; European;

LA 2448: Tewa Polychrome, Tewa Polished Red, Tewa (Kapo) Polished Black, Zia Polychrome.

Settlement in the Agua Fria area west of Santa Fe would appear, on the basis of the ceramic types recorded in the Laboratory of Anthropology, to fall into two time periods: a pre-A.D. 1450 and a post-A.D. 1550 occupation. Here, as in Santa Fe, the middle and later types in the Rio Grande glaze series are poorly represented. If we can take this underrepresentation as evidence of absence of settlement rather than sampling error, then at Agua Fria as well as at Santa Fe, Arroyo Hondo Pueblo, and the area around the Lamy cutoff there seems to have been an occupational gap from the Middle Classic Period to the Historic Period.

References

ADAMS, ROBERT M.
1962   "Agriculture and Urban Life in Early Southwestern Iran," *Science* 136:109–22.
BINFORD, L. R., S. R. BINFORD, R. WHALLON, AND M. A. HARDIN
1970   *Archaeology at Hatchery West*, Memoirs of the Society for American Archaeology 24 (Washington, D.C.).
BIRDSELL, J. B.
1957   "Some Population Problems Involving Pleistocene Man," Cold Spring Harbor Symposia on Quantitative Biology 22:47–69.
BOSERUP, ESTHER
1965   *The Conditions of Agricultural Growth* (Chicago: Aldine Publishing Company).
BOUGHLEY, ARTHUR S.
1968   *Ecology of Populations* (London: Macmillan and Company).
BRADFIELD, MAITLAND
1971   *The Changing Pattern of Hopi Agriculture*, Royal Anthropological Institute of Great Britain and Ireland, Occasional Papers no. 30 (London).
BRETERNITZ, DAVID A.
1966   *An Appraisal of Tree-Ring Dated Pottery in the Southwest*, Anthropological Papers of the University of Arizona no. 10 (Tucson).
BRYSON, REID A., AND PAUL R. JULIAN
1962   *Proceedings of the Conference on the Climate of the Eleventh and Sixteenth Centuries, Aspen, Colorado, June 16–24, 1962*, High Altitude Observatory of the National Center for Atmospheric Research, Scientific Report no. 1 (Boulder).
CARTER, GEORGE F.
1945   *Plant Geography and Culture History in the American Southwest*, Viking Fund Publications in Anthropology no. 5 (New York).
CLARKE, DAVID L.
1968   *Analytical Archaeology* (London: Methuen and Company).

127

COE, M. D., AND K. V. FLANNERY
1966   "Microenvironments and Mesoamerican Prehistory," in *New Roads to Yes-terday*, ed. J. R. Caldwell (New York: Basic Books).
1967   *Early Cultures and Human Ecology in South Coastal Guatemala*, Smith-sonian Institution Contributions to Anthropology, vol. 3 (Washington, D.C.).
DICKSON, D. BRUCE
1975   "Settlement Pattern Stability and Change in the Middle Northern Rio Grande Region, New Mexico: A Test of Some Hypotheses," *American Antiquity* 40:159–71.
DITTERT, A. E., JR., J. J. HESTER, AND F. W. EDDY
1961   *An Archaeological Survey of the Navajo Reservoir District, Northwestern New Mexico*, School of American Research Monograph no. 23 (Santa Fe, N.M.).
FORD, J. A.
1949   "Cultural Dating of Prehistoric Sites in the Viru Valley, Peru," *Anthropological Papers of the American Museum of Natural History* 43:29–89 (New York).
FORD, RICHARD
1972   "An Ecological Perspective on the Eastern Pueblos," in *New Perspectives on the Pueblos*, ed. Alfonso Ortiz, School of American Research Advanced Seminar Series (Albuquerque: University of New Mexico Press).
FORD, R. I., A. H. SCHROEDER, AND S. L. PECKHAM
1972   "Three Perspectives on Puebloan History," in *New Perspectives on the Pueblos*, ed. Alfonso Ortiz, School of American Research Advanced Seminar Series (Albuquerque: University of New Mexico Press).
FORDE, C. D.
1931   "Hopi Agriculture and Land Ownership," *Journal of the Royal Anthropological Institute of Great Britain and Ireland* 61:357–405.
FRITTS, H. C.
1965   "Tree Ring Evidence for Climatic Changes in Western North America," *Monthly Weather Review* 93:431–43.
GERKINS, SHELBY D.
1969   *Biological Systems* (Philadelphia: W. B. Saunders Co.).
GLADWIN, H. S.
1945   *The Chaco Branch: Excavations at White Mound and in the Red Mesa Valley*, Medallion Papers no. 33 (Globe, Arizona).
GLADWIN, H. S., E. W. HAURY, E. B. SAYLES, AND NORA GLADWIN
1937   *Excavations at Snaketown: I, Material Culture*, Medallion Papers no. 25 (Globe, Arizona).
GLASSOW, MICHAEL A.
1971   Review of "Early Puebloan Occupations at Tesuque By-Pass and in the Upper Rio Grande Valley," by Charles H. McNutt, *American Antiquity* 36:225–26.
HACK, JOHN T.
1942   *The Changing Physical Environment of the Hopi Indians of Arizona*, Papers of the Peabody Museum of American Archaeology and Ethnology, vol. 35 (Cambridge, Mass.).
HAMMOND, NORMAN D.C.
1972   "Locational Models and the Site of Lubaantun: a Classic Maya Centre," in *Models in Archaeology*, ed. David L. Clarke (London: Methuen & Co., Ltd.).

128

References

HAURY, EMIL W.
1936   "The Snaketown Canal," University of New Mexico Bulletin, Anthropological Series 1 (Albuquerque).
HOLDRIDGE, L. R.
1964   Life-Zone Ecology (San Jose, Costa Rica: Tropical Science Center).
HOLE, FRANK, K. V. FLANNERY, AND J. A. NEELY
1969   Prehistory and Human Ecology of the Deh Luran Plain, University of Michigan Museum of Anthropology Memoir no. 1 (Ann Arbor).
JOHNSON, ALFRED E.
1960   "The Place of the Trincheras Culture of Northern Sonora in Southwestern Archaeology," manuscript, Department of Anthropology, University of Arizona (Tucson).
JUDGE, W. J.
1973   PaleoIndian Occupation of the Central Rio Grande Valley, New Mexico (Albuquerque: University of New Mexico Press).
KELLEY, N. EDMUND
1980   The Present-Day Ecology of Arroyo Hondo, New Mexico, Arroyo Hondo Archaeological Series, vol. 1 (Santa Fe: School of American Research Press).
KIDDER, ALFRED V.
1915   "Pottery of the Pajarito Plateau and of Some Adjacent Regions of New Mexico," American Anthropological Association Memoir no. 21, pp. 407–620.
1927   "Southwestern Archaeological Conference," El Palacio 23:554–61.
LANGE, CHARLES H.
1968   The Cochiti Dam Archaeological Salvage Project, Part I: Report on the 1963 Season, Museum of New Mexico Research Records no. 6 (Santa Fe).
LARSON, LEWIS H.
1972   "Functional Considerations of Warfare in the Southeast During the Mississippian Period," American Antiquity 37:383–92.
MCNUTT, CHARLES
1969   Early Puebloan Occupations at Tesuque By-Pass and in the Upper Rio Grande Valley, University of Michigan Museum of Anthropology Papers no. 40 (Ann Arbor).
MERA, H. P.
1935   Ceramic Clues to the Prehistory of North Central New Mexico, Laboratory of Anthropology Technical Series Bulletin no. 8 (Santa Fe).
NELSON, N. C.
1914   Pueblo Ruins of the Galisteo Basin, New Mexico, Anthropological Papers of the American Museum of Natural History no. 15 (New York).
NIETSCHMANN, BERNARD
1972   "Hunting and Fishing among the Miskito Indians, Eastern Nicaragua," Human Ecology 1:41–67.
PECKHAM, STEWART L., AND J. WILSON
n.d.   "An Archaeological Survey of the Chuska Valley, New Mexico," manuscript, Museum of New Mexico, Laboratory of Anthropology (Santa Fe).
PHILLIPS, PHILIP, JAMES A. FORD, AND JAMES B. GRIFFIN
1951   Archaeological Survey in the Lower Mississippi Alluvial Valley, 1940–46, Papers of the Peabody Museum of American Archaeology and Ethnology no. 25 (Cambridge, Mass.).
PLOG, FRED
1975   "Demographic Studies in Southwestern Prehistory," in Population Studies

in Archaeology and Biological Anthropology: A Symposium, ed. A. C. Swed-
lund, Society for American Archaeology Memoir no. 30.

REDMAN, CHARLES L., AND PATTY JO WATSON
1970   "Systematic, Intensive Surface Collection," *American Antiquity* 35:279–91.

REED, ERIK K.
1949   "Sources of Upper Rio Grande Culture and Population," *El Palacio* 56:163–
        84.

REINHART, T. R.
1968   "Late Archaic Cultures of the Middle Rio Grande Valley, New Mexico"
        (Ph.D. diss., University of New Mexico).

RILEY, CARROLL L.
1952   "San Juan Anasazi and the Galisteo Basin," *El Palacio* 59:77–82.

ROBINSON, WILLIAM J., BRUCE G. HARRILL, AND RICHARD L. WARREN
1973   *Tree-Ring Dates from New Mexico J-K, P, V: Santa Fe-Pecos-Lincoln Area*,
        Laboratory of Tree-Ring Research, University of Arizona (Tucson).

ROHN, A. H.
1963   "Prehistoric Soil and Water Conservation on Chapin Mesa," *American An-
        tiquity* 28:65–69.

ROWE, JOHN H.
1961   "Stratigraphy and Seriation," *American Antiquity* 26:324–30.
1962   "Stages and Periods in Archaeological Interpretation," *Southwestern Journal
        of Anthropology* 18:40–54.

SCHOENWETTER, JAMES, AND ALFRED E. DITTERT, JR.
1968   "An Ecological Interpretation of Anasazi Settlement Patterns," in *An-
        thropological Archaeology in the Americas*, ed. Betty J. Meggers (Washing-
        ton, D.C.: Anthropological Society of Washington).

SCHWARTZ, DOUGLAS W.
1956   "Demographic Changes in the Early Period of Cohonina Prehistory," in *Pre-
        historic Settlement Patterns in the New World*, ed. Gordon Willey, Viking
        Fund Publications in Anthropology no. 23:26–31 (New York).
1970   "Cultural and Ecological Ramifications of Population Growth," research
        proposal submitted to the National Science Foundation (Santa Fe: School of
        American Research).

SCHWARTZ, DOUGLAS W., AND RICHARD W. LANG
1973   *Archaeological Investigations at the Arroyo Hondo Site: Third Field Report*,
        1972 (Santa Fe: School of American Research).

SEARS, WILLIAM H.
1964   "The Southeastern United States," in *Prehistoric Man in the New World*, ed.
        Jesse Jennings and E. Norbeck (Chicago: University of Chicago Press).

SHELFORD, VICTOR E.
1963   *The Ecology of North America* (Urbana, Ill.: University of Illinois Press).

SIMPSON, J. H.
1850   *Journal of a Military Reconnaissance from Santa Fe, New Mexico, to the
        Navajo Country*, Report of the Secretary of War, 31st Congress, 1st Session
        (Washington, D.C.).

SMILEY, TERAH L., S. A. STUBBS, AND BRYANT BANNISTER
1953   *A Foundation for the Dating of Some Late Archaeological Sites in the Rio
        Grande Area, New Mexico*, Laboratory of Tree-Ring Research, Tree-Ring
        Bulletin no. 6 (Tucson).

References

SPIEGEL, ZANE, AND BREWSTER BALDWIN
1963   *Geology and Water Resources of the Santa Fe Area, New Mexico*, U.S. Geological Survey Water Supply Paper no. 1525 (Washington, D.C.).

STEWART, GUY R., AND MAURICE DONNELLY
1943   "Soil and Water Economy in the Pueblo Southwest," *Science Monthly* 56:31–44, 134–44.

STUBBS, STANLEY, AND W. S. STALLINGS
1953   *The Excavation of Pindi Pueblo, New Mexico*, School of American Research Monograph no. 18 (Santa Fe).

TUGGLE, HAROLD D.
1970   "Prehistoric Community-Relationships in East Central Arizona," (Ph.D. diss., University of Arizona).

VIVIAN, GWINN R.
1970   "An Inquiry into Prehistoric Social Organization in Chaco Canyon, New Mexico," in *Reconstructing Prehistoric Pueblo Societies*, ed. W. A. Longacre, School of American Research Advanced Seminar Series (Albuquerque: University of New Mexico Press).

WENDORF, FRED
1953   *Salvage Archaeology in the Chama Valley, New Mexico*, School of American Research Monograph no. 17 (Santa Fe).
1954   "A Reconstruction of Northern Rio Grande Prehistory," *American Anthropologist* 56:200–227.

WENDORF, FRED, AND JOHN P. MILLER
1959   "Artifacts from High Mountain Sites in the Sangre de Cristo Range, New Mexico," *El Palacio* 66:37–52.

WENDORF, FRED, AND ERIK K. REED
1955   "An Alternative Reconstruction of Northern Rio Grande Prehistory," *El Palacio* 62:131–73.

WETHERINGTON, RONALD K.
1968   *Excavations at Pot Creek Pueblo*, Fort Burgwin Research Center Publication no. 6 (Taos, N. M.).

WHITING, ALFRED F.
1939   *Ethnobotany of the Hopi*, Museum of Northern Arizona Bulletin no. 15 (Flagstaff).

ZUBROW, E. B. W.
1971   "Carrying Capacity and Dynamic Equilibrium in the Prehistoric Southwest," *American Antiquity* 36:127–38.

131

12227569R00097

Made in the USA
Lexington, KY
02 December 2011